Soli Deo Gloria

Martin

KORNELIS
MISKOTTE

Kornelis Miskotte

KORNELIS MISKOTTE

A Biblical Theology

Martin Kessler

Selinsgrove: Susquehanna University Press
London: Associated University Presses

Associated University Presses
440 Forsgate Drive
Cranbury, NJ 08512

Associated University Presses
16 Barter Street
London WC1A 2AH, England

Associated University Presses
P.O. Box 338, Port Credit
Mississauga, Ontario
Canada L5G 4L8

The paper used in this publication meets the requirements of the American National Standard for Permanence of Paper for Printed Library Materials Z39.48–1984.

Library of Congress Cataloging-in-Publication Data

Kessler, Martin, 1927–
Kornelis Miskotte : a biblical theology / Martin Kessler.
p. cm.
Includes bibliographical references and index.
ISBN 1-57591-000-4 (alk. paper)
1. Miskotte, Kornelis Heiko, 1894–1976. 2. Reformed Church—Doctrines—History—20th century. 3. Theology—Netherlands—History—20th century. I. Title.
BX9479.M57K47 1997
230'.42'092—dc20 96-30265
CIP

PRINTED IN THE UNITED STATES OF AMERICA

Affectionately dedicated to
our children:
Nancy, John, Marjorie & Stephen, Nadine & Elmer

Contents

Preface

THE IMMEDIATE PREDECESSOR OF THIS WORK IS AN ACADEMIC THEsis, in partial fulfilment for the requirements of the STM degree at Lutheran Theological Seminary, Gettysburg, Pennsylvania, under the tutelage of Professor Eric Crump. But its origins go back much farther.

While still living in the Netherlands, I vaguely remember when Miskotte, in 1945, demonstratively joined the Dutch Labor Party, together with some of his friends, also ministers in the Dutch Reformed Church. That action sent something of a shock wave through the country. It was called "doorbraak" [breakthrough]. Church people did not do such things! They had their own political parties: Roman Catholics had theirs, and Protestants had three or four parties to choose from.

Later, while serving a congregation in Toronto (in 1960), a Dutch parishioner told me of his enthusiasm for "Dominee Buskes" (The Rev. Dr. J. J. Buskes), an Amsterdam friend and colleague of Miskotte, and another one of the "red pastors." In early March of 1970, I heard Dr. Buskes preach in the Westerkerk in Amsterdam, a short distance from the Anne Frank House.

In 1968, while serving on the faculty of Clarkson University in Potsdam, New York, I saw Miskotte's book *When the Gods are Silent*. A cursory glance convinced me that I should not attempt to read it, since neither time nor a tutor were available.

A stimulating course at Lutheran Seminary, Gettysburg, on 19th century atheism (Fall, 1992) by Professor Crump revived my memory of and interest in Miskotte, which eventually led to the present work. My thanks go to him!

The study of Miskotte is challenging but rewards the effort. With Miskotte I experienced a theological housecleaning (Miskotte might have chuckled and called it "removing the rubbish!"), and many ideas introduced by my Amsterdam friends (Old Testament scholars), who also profess their indebtedness to Miskotte, came into clearer focus.

The experience was a feast for me. Miskotte seemed a refreshing Garden of Eden compared to what one is apt to find at the "left" or the "right" of the theological spectrum. Miskotte comes across not as a "hyphenated" but as a biblical theologian. His theses resonate. But there is more: Beyond the intellectual that he was, Miskotte was, as we might put it, a man of God to whom the pastorate was totally serious business. He unstintingly gave his talents to the service of Christ and his church and served with great devotion even when the going was rough or when he suffered personal tragedy. Miskotte modeled a unique combination of scholarship and faith (one of his collections of essays is aptly called *Geloof en Kennis* [Faith and Knowledge]) that inspires one to emulation.

He is no longer with us but his work remains; in fact, it seems to experience a veritable renaissance in the Netherlands, where 1994, the centennial year of his birth, was remembered with symposiums and lectures about his work. One hopes that the relatively poor reception of *When the Gods are Silent* in the English-speaking world may be superseded by a revival of interest in what this teacher of the church contributed, like old wine that improves with age. He has much to say to the present theological scene!

May this small beginning, then, in its modest way be an impetus toward increasing interest in Miskotte and what he stood for. A reprint is needed of *When the Gods are Silent.* Others of his works (such as his *Bijbels ABC*) merit an English translation; finally, an anthology of some of his writings, published in English, may find an appreciative readership.

Last but not least, I wish to offer sincere thanks to several people who have in various ways taught, supported, and encouraged me in this work: my professor/supervisor, Prof. Dr. Eric H. Crump of Gettysburg Seminary, for his constant inspiration in this project, Prof. Dr. Christopher R. Seitz, Yale University, for his spirited encouragement of my Miskotte research; and in The Netherlands, two children of Dr. Miskotte: Ms. E. Kuiper-Miskotte, for a delightful and informative interview and Prof. Dr. H. H. Miskotte; for his help in "finding the way" among sources on Miskotte; Ms. Christiane Berkvens-Stevelinck, Curator, Section "Westerse handschriften," Universiteitsbibliotheek, Leiden, for help with some of Miskotte's manuscripts; Prof. Dr. Karel A. Deurloo, University of Amsterdam, for his constant inspiration as a "father and brother" in all of my researches in Old Testament; Drs. F. H. Hoogewoud of the Rosenthaliana Library, Amsterdam, for his reliable friendship and helpfulness in many crucial details; the Rev. Dr. Dirk Monshouwer, Pastor, and Director of The Miskotte Foundation, for permission to print in English translation three articles from Prof. Miskotte's works, and finally, to the Susquehanna University Press, Selinsgrove, Pennsylvania, for accepting this work for publication.

* * *

The pronouns "he," "his," and "him" are used sparingly throughout this text to enhance communication. They are not meant to indicate gender or offend any reader.

Introduction

THERE CAN BE NO DOUBT THAT KORNELIS MISKOTTE SHOULD BE classified as a Barthian. While Miskotte was in his first parish for only a few years, he was introduced for the first time to Barth. His initial and subsequent reaction is described in Chapter 1. As time went on, he became an ardent defender of Barth, and at one time even wrote three articles polemicizing against those who wanted to leave Barth behind.

As has been pointed out with some completeness by Muis in his excellent dissertation, however, Miskotte also illustrates a number of independent developments which Muis touched on in his paper.

As a Barthian and a well-read philosopher, Miskotte was not in the business of what evangelicals call "apologetics." He was, as Neven indicated, a post "God-is-dead" theologian. Faith does not need ontological foundations; he constantly downplays the classical attributes such as omnipotence, omniscience, and omnipresence. With Barth, he believes that God addresses humankind in the Word (of the Scriptures).

In Chapter 2 an attempt is made to sketch his intellectual/theological pedigree. We take a closer look at what made this man tick as an intellectual and a theologian, hopefully without falling into the trap of oversimplification. That is not simple, for Miskotte was indeed a very complex man, in whose presence most of us feel like pygmies. The discussion that follows has attempted to sketch first and foremost: Miskotte the man, the pastor, the theologian.

The remainder of this work consists of two blocks of two chapters each. "Church and Synagogue" (Chapter 3) and "Religion, Paganism, and Nihilism" (Chapter 4) belong together. Miskotte, already in his *Edda en Thora* (1939) spoke of the three groups on which he focused his scholarly attention, namely pagans, Jews, and Christians. While that work reflects the temper of the thirties, a time of foreboding, we live in an era where much of such foreboding has been realized. Even so, Miskotte's work is a brilliant analysis of paganism vis-à-vis the religion of the Bible (Torah).

Miskotte's novelty was that he, as a Christian theologian, took Judaism seriously as an independent faith. His statement in the opening sentences of his Groningen dissertion, *Het Wezen der Joodse Religie* (1932), strikes the keynote not only of this important work, but of his theology as a whole.

Finally, in his third and final opus, the forerunner of the English translation *When the Gods are Silent* (1956), he directs his searchlight on the nihilist-Christian dialogue. For him, Christianity is misguided when it focuses solely or even mainly on the New Testament. In this work, which sets forth more completely than any other work his view of Scripture, he states that we need to begin with the Old Testament, then turn to the New Testament, and finally, return to the Old Testament. The tongue-in-cheek anecdote by Tom Naastepad at Frans Breukelman's party about "the perfect Bible" being an Old Testament with all of the New Testament added in footnotes, is Miskottean in spirit.

From *When the Gods are Silent,* as well as from his work *Om het levende Woord* (1948), which had a rather long history, we learn about his contact with the Bible. One point he keeps reiterating is to let it speak for itself. Indeed, whatever we may say of Miskotte, first and foremost he tried to be a biblical theologian. Many theologians make this claim of course, but the problem is that many of them, in common with non-theological scholars, have difficulty reading without undue interference from their own presuppositions. One of Miskotte's unmistakable skills was that he knew how to read, how to absorb what he read, and how to integrate it with "his system." Of course, he paid the price for such intense intellectual preoccupation. In this paper, a few glimpses from his personal emotional life have been shared. In the *dagboeken* [diaries], which are an invaluable source of his life, we find much more of the same. The sheer load of what he had read and absorbed must occasionally have overburdened him. That is without question the reason why it took him so long to "get his act together." The simpleton has no such problems, but the genius is bound to be terribly frustrated.

The final two-chapter block is "The Old Testament" (Chapter 5) and "The Biblical ABCs" (Chapter 6). These two chapters also belong together. The "surplus" treats his Old Testament teaching under several heads, as does the selection made from the biblical ABCs. Taken together, they should offer some insight of Miskotte's approach to the Old Testament. It is quite remarkable how relevant his comments still are, in spite of the fact that *Bijbels ABC* originated in Bible discussion groups in the winter of 1940/41, the first winter of the Nazi occupation. This work proceeds phenomenologically, unlike *When the Gods are Silent,* which is conceived dialogically and systematically. The contributions of both are shared in this work.

Finally, by way of a bonus for patient readers, three appendices are added; they are samples from: *Edda en Torah* (Chapter 1), *Bijbels ABC* (Chapter 9), and "The Presence and Future of Israel" (Miskotte's exposition of Article 17 of the proposed Dutch Reformed Confession, in *De kern van de zaak,* 1950). The latter work has been described as the closest thing Miskotte has to offer that resembles a dogmatics.

Happy reading!

KORNELIS MISKOTTE

1
Miskotte the Man

THE NAME KORNELIS HEIKO MISKOTTE IS HARDLY A HOUSEHOLD word in the field of theology or philosophy. In the United States he is barely known. His magnum opus, *Wenn die Götter schweigen*,[1] translated as *When the Gods are Silent*,[2] received only superficial reviews in the United States.[3] The *Oxford Dictionary of the Christian Church* betrays its (Anglo-Saxon) provincialism in its limited coverage beyond the English-speaking world; Karl Barth, Emil Brunner, and Nathan Söderblom are featured in brief articles but Miskotte, whom many would consider to be in the same league, does not even get an entry.[4]

However, Dr. Miskotte is considered a major twentieth-century theologian in the Netherlands (where the centennial of his birth was celebrated in 1994) and to a lesser degree in Germany. A number of his works, or studies about him, have been translated, or have originally been written in German.[5] Dutch dissertations on Miskotte are still being written,[6] and students are exposed to his teachings.[7] It is reported that he is required reading among theological students in New Zealand.[8]

Who was Miskotte? He was a man of many talents, but he would surely want to be remembered above all in the classical Reformed way as "pastor and teacher."[9] R. Zuurmond (Professor, University of Amsterdam) characterizes him as "pastor and scribe, poet and philosopher—in short, theologian."[10] Deurloo would add catechist and letter-writer[11] and Karl Barth, seer and poet.[12] He was born September 23, 1894, in Utrecht, the heart of the Netherlands, of Saxon parents; his father came from an old farmer's family in the province of Overijsel and his mother grew up in a Dutch Reformed parsonage in Den Ham, in central Overijsel. His parents moved to Utrecht after they were married, and Kornelis Heiko was their first child.

Youth and Education

Kornelis attended public schools and a Christian Gymnasium where he read what he could get his hands on: theology, philosophy, but especially poets and novelists. The fairly complete diaries which he kept for most of his life fill in many of the details of the life of this complex man.[13]

He dates his call to the ministry to a meeting in the Dom Church at Utrecht, at age ten. He attended catechism classes since before he knew how to read, and was not confirmed until he was twenty-one years old. Apparently, his catechism teachers made quite an impression on him.[14]

His university training (at Utrecht) was hardly inspiring in terms of his intellectual development. He mentions only two theology professors, and neither was a biblical or theological expert.[15] Since his diaries give us many pictures of his personal intellectual and spiritual life (even while leaving many gaps!), we learn that among the many names mentioned, two stand out as the chief figures in his initial theological development: Hermann Friedrich Kohlbrügge (1803–1875)[16] and Johannes Hermanus Gunning (1829–1905). Later, Karl Barth became the dominant influence in his theological evolution.[17] In fact, he is widely regarded as the Dutch interpreter of Barth: loyal, but independent. However, he drank from a variety of wells. All during his life he was fond of poetry; Guido Gezelle, a Flemish poet, remained a favorite with him. Not only poets (several of them) did Miskotte read, but also theologians, philosophers, and other writers. After his death, when some university librarians inspected his library, they were surprised to learn that the overwhelming majority of his books were literary works.[18] He was a voracious reader. His son, author of a delightful book about his father's life and work (see note 10), wrote: "I believe that he read differently from most people, unusually concentrated and quickly. In a short time he was able to penetrate to the thrust [kern] of difficult texts and make them completely his own."[19] This is an important point to be borne in mind in connection with our search for the sources of his thought, to be discussed in chapter 2.

Career Struggles

In his student years Miskotte often lamented that he had accomplished so little[20]—a note that keeps recurring during his lifetime for he was something of a perfectionist. He could not settle on a dissertation topic (see Chapter 2, "Dissertation Topic"). During his student days he did considerable agonizing about his career. On February 21, 1919, he wrote some introspective comments in his diary about his future: "Often I wonder in which field I would be a pioneer . . . [but] I search without the serious will to find; I realize that I am too original to be led and too multisided and appreciative to be able to lead." Then the idea of the pastorate came to him. This more or less stuck after he thought of other careers. Besides, some other activities would be compatible with the pastorate. Rather than exercising himself too much about his doctorate at that point, he wrote that he wanted to become a "culturally mature [man], not a professional or a specialist." What he needed, he wrote, was "time to mature, time to round off my studies, time . . . to 'find' a wife."

The Pastorate

On Tuesday, February 1, 1921, his call to serve the church at Cortgene (presently spelled Kortgene), in the province of Zeeland arrived. He reflected: "One cannot do anything else but remain with the people and at the same time near the Bible. . . . I become responsible for the act of speaking. I have little else but my love for Jesus, who promised another world but [regret] that I have to leave my football matches for good. . . ."

On May 22, 1921, he was installed in his first pastorate, a congregation with 1,350 members. He hardly fit in with the provincialism of his parishioners but he diligently applied himself to his pastoral labors. We have a remarkable record of some of his pastoral writings in his parish newsletter which has been republished under the title *. . . als een die dient* [. . . as one who serves].[21] The title is based on Luke 22:27: "but I am among you as one who serves," which was the text of his first sermon at Cortgene. Other pastorates followed: Meppel (1925–1930), in the province of Drente,[22] Haarlem (a short distance west of Amsterdam), 1930–1938, and finally, Amsterdam (1938–1945), from where he was called as "ecclesiastical professor" to the University of Leiden where he served until his retirement in 1959.

His time at Haarlem was particularly fruitful.[23] Touw summarizes the situation as follows: "This point of time was in many respects extremely exciting for the church and the world. The Netherlands experienced a growing spiritual and social crisis with the rise of the newer theology and the struggle for a new church order, while Germany witnessed the rise of national-socialism and anti-Semitism. Increasingly, Miskotte provided spiritual leadership, and contributed uniquely to the spiritual renewal of the church."[24]

All during his career, Miskotte held that the ministry should not only provide for worship, but also for learning; right beside the church, in Jewish fashion, there must be the bêt midraš, the house of learning. Thus, he organized what would be called today "Bible studies." Thanks to the care and diligence of his Haarlem parishioners, some of these studies were transcribed and eventually published: most significantly, those on Ruth and Job.[25]

Dissertation Plans

During his Haarlem period, Miskotte also completed his dissertation (in 1932, at Groningen University), entitled: *Het Wezen der Joodsche Religie. Vergelijkende studie over de voornaamste structuren der Joodsche Godsdienstphilosophie van dezen tijd* [The Nature of Jewish Religion. Comparative Study of the Most Significant Structures of Contemporary Jewish Philosophy of Religion].[26] He graduated cum laude and received the Mallinckrodt prize in 1935 for the best theological dissertation of the decade. The subject of his dissertation was something of a surprise, not the least to Jews.[27] It was reprinted in 1964 (with a revised subtitle: *Bijdrage tot de kennis van het Joodse geestesleven* [Contribution to the Knowledge of Jewish Intellectual Life]) and has also been reprinted as Verzameld Werk 6 (see chapters 2, "Dissertation Topic" and 3, "The Dissertation.")

Battling Nazism

In 1938 Miskotte began his ministry in Amsterdam. The following year saw the publication of his book *Edda en Thora. Een vergelijking van Germaansche en Israëlitische religie* [Edda and Torah. A Comparison of Germanic and Israelite Religion].[28] In this work, the Sitz im Leben of which is the growing conflict between Christianity and (German) National Socialism, the myths and epics of the ancient

German Edda were contrasted with the Old Testament. Miskotte was convinced that German National Socialism was reflected in the songs of the Edda.

Miskotte continued his prewar anti-Nazism stance during the German occupation of the Netherlands (1940–1945). During that time Miskotte wrote an illegal pamphlet entitled "Better Resistance."[29] But his most significant anti-Nazi writing was his *Bijbels ABC*,[30] a little book packing a big punch, with its discussions of a number of key words in the Bible, e.g., the name, the acts of God, the word, the way, etc. (See chapter 6.)

While he had been happy in Haarlem, unquestionably the most fruitful and happiest years of his career were spent in the ministry in Amsterdam. On September 25, 1938, he was installed in the Westerkerk, a stone's throw from the Anne Frank House. Five years later Miskotte received a special charge from the Amsterdam Church Consistory to work among the unchurched in (more prosperous) Southern Amsterdam.

After the War: Leiden and Church Reform

When the Netherlands were liberated, Miskotte was heard preaching in the Nieuwe Kerk (on The Dam) in Amsterdam on May 9, 1945, on the text: "God's enemies shall perish" (Psalm 92:9a). The prayers offered in that service found a permanent place in the *Dienstboek* [Service Book] of the Dutch Reformed Church.[31] In the following month seven Dutch Reformed pastors in Amsterdam (Miskotte among them) joined the Dutch Socialist party (S.D.A.P.). This move, which had been brewing for many years, must be seen from within the Dutch religio-political context.[32]

In August 1945, Miskotte was named Ecclesiastical Professor at Leiden University (by the General Synod of the Dutch Reformed Church).[33] His charge was dogmatics, ethics, ecclesiastical law, and missions. He left his parish with mixed feelings. "In Amsterdam he found a marvelous openness and gratitude for his word during the dark years of the occupation, which particularly inspired him to offer his manifold gifts at the service of seekers. 'He never felt happier in any other place,'" a friend wrote.[34]

In October 1945, the same month when Miskotte took his Leiden professorship, the General Synod of the Dutch Reformed Church convened for the first time in three centuries. At the eve of the synodical gathering, Miskotte led a prayer service in the Nieuwe Kerk, where he preached on the text: "One thing is needed" (Luke 10:42). Touw summarizes as follows: "One thing is needed, namely to sit at the feet of Jesus, to hear his word. . . . Today, if you hear his voice, do not harden your heart, you activists who are so swift with words, you introverts who guard the truth and are so occupied with yourself . . . all of you who hear and understand, bow down, and receive, in Christ's name, the one thing that is needed."[35]

A year after he began his professorship, Miskotte suffered a profound personal tragedy. At the wedding dinner for a former catechumen who had married a Jewish girl whom the Miskottes had hidden from the Nazis during the war, signs of severe food poisoning appeared, claiming the lives of Mrs. Miskotte, their daughter Alma, and the groom. The other Miskotte children remained in danger for several weeks. At one of the graves, Miskotte said: "I stand here, borne by God's faithfulness and strengthened in the Spirit . . . but I am not a hero, or a hero of faith, and I thank God, that I do not need to be. May the strong Hero whom God chose, assist us."[36]

Miskotte was blessed with many gifts and at this stage of his career at any rate, the church made good use of them. In 1951 he was made Chairman of the Commission for a new translation of the rhymed Psalter of the Reformed Church, replacing the 1773 version. The membership of the Commission consisted of Old Testament scholars, musical experts, plus eight well-known poets. In 1958, a provisional edition with 110 psalms was published. Three years later, another provisional edition came out, containing all 150 psalms, and in 1968 the definitive edition saw the light. It became the first part of a song book[37] (the second part contains 491 hymns, several of them newly composed) which was adopted by five Dutch Protestant denominations (including the Lutherans and the Mennonites).

Magnum Opus

The greatest of his major works, his magnum opus *Als de goden zwijgen,* was published in 1956[38] while the English translation, *When the Gods are Silent,* came out in 1967. It has been characterized as a triptych. The first part: "A Mirror of Our Times" [Kleine Zeitspiegel] offers a rich sketch of the thought of the time. The "fourth man" (perhaps comparable to Bonhoeffer's "man come of age") is defined as "the man who no longer believes, in the biblical sense of the term . . . but he is equally deaf to other gods and free from the binding power of godlike values. He is the man who no longer responds to any spiritual appeal. He lacks even the ability to do so."[39]

The second part, "Witness and Interpretation," tries to show why modern man experiences liberation if he would listen to the Old Testament. Chapter 1, entitled "Tensions," deals with attitudes toward the Old Testament: some have little sympathy toward it, have a problem recognizing it as Scripture (which is related to anti-Semitism), whereas the Old Testament has also been the target of rationalist interpretations. Finally, there is the church-synagogue schism. The next section discusses *compromises* and contains attempts at describing the meaning of the Old Testament, by means of "schemata" such as *law and gospel* (which, for Miskotte, misunderstands and distorts both testaments) and *prophecy and fulfilment* (which is also less than satisfactory). Miskotte concludes that the tensions between the testaments cannot be eliminated by religious and rational distinctions.

The next section, "The Oneness of the Times," discusses revelation. The Scripture is the word about the Word of the WORD: saying, event, and salvation belong together. Without proposing another schema, Miskotte speaks of expectation (in the Old Testament) and recollection (in the New Testament). The Covenant is about the God of the Bible: his character, attitude, and action. It points to his elective grace. Human violation of the covenant is rebellion against God. It is the subject of preaching. Pinpointing this discussion, Miskotte next turns to a crucial subject: the Name, referring to Exod 3:14: אהיה אשר אהיה. The affirmation: "YHWH is God" is irreversible: this is crucial. Miskotte does not put "essence" before "truth"; that would make God into a humanly constructed idea!

In the section "The anthropomorphous Name" Miskotte stresses hearing before seeing; the intermediate stage is anthropomorphism (as in preaching). This is the sequence of divine revelation. Thus, Chapter 1 moves from tensions to (false) compromises, via "oneness of the times"—which describe, as it were, the conditions for revelation, to "the Name" which is the heart of revelation.

Chapter 2 outlines the "givenness" or the qualities of what is given [Gegebenheiten]. Creation is opposed to eternal becoming; this is the first of a series of opposites. Miskotte seems to accept Thorleif Boman's *Hebrew Thought Compared with Greek* (see n.45, chap. 5). Preaching needs to take seriously the Israelite idiom of Scripture; we need to move from the particular (concrete) to the universal (essence) and not vice versa. This also means that we need to watch our translation, as well as our understanding of biblical (Hebrew) words. Interpreting the Bible Israelitically also means for Miskotte that we use the Hebrew order of books. The Torah contains the witness of God's revelation. The Prophets recall Israel to the covenant and the commandment. The Writings describe how the community reacts to divine revelation. This discussion leads directly to "Exegesis." Christological interpretation is a testimony but is actually a pious "reinterpretation" and as such inadmissible. Miskotte takes a low profile on hermeneutics; since the Bible is a human book, we need only to listen to what it has to say to us. When the Word comes to us, then the heart—that includes understanding, will, feeling, and imagination [Einbildungskraft]—is kindled by hearing the address of God, by "knowing" God. This is strictly unique with Miskotte. Once more, Miskotte turns to the schema "Promise and Fulfilment." We must not read Christ into the Old Testament; rather, we need to learn from the Old Testament what the Christ means. But there is also the parting of the ways; Jews have the Talmud as their sequel to the Old Testament.

The third chapter of Part II is entitled "The Surplus." Miskotte regards the Old Testament as the "fundamental first part" of the Bible, containing both a deficit and a surplus. As to the deficit, the love of God is proclaimed, but the word is seldom used; it is overshadowed by his sovereign power. Comments on "The Surplus" (173–302) are found in chapter 5.

Part III, "Examples of an Application," contains fourteen homiletical sketches on Old Testament texts for preaching (375–460) beginning with Psalm 100 (Universal Praise), then three selections from Exodus dealing with revelation, two selections on "newness," four selections narrating the story of Jonah, the reluctant prophet, and ending with "Light is Sweet" (Eccl. 11:7).

Touw speaks in terms of a trilogy of Miskotte's works: *Wezen der Joodse Religie* (1932), *Edda en Thora* (1949), and *When the Gods are Silent* (1956/1963/1967).[40] Others would include in the list of his "major works": *Om het levende woord. Opstellen over de praktijk der exegese* [Concerning the Living Word. Essays about the Practice of Exegesis].[41]

Conclusion

Miskotte's literary output will be referred to repeatedly in the remainder of this study, beginning with a closer look at the sources of his thought in Chapter 2. Perhaps a good way to close this chapter may be to quote a most eloquent accolade about him, which sums up "the man Miskotte." It was written by Hinrich Stoevesandt[42] who has contributed greatly to the dissemination of Miskotte's work by serving as translator and editor of most of Miskotte's publications in German:[43] "Miskotte was theologian with heart and soul. However, he was at the same time, in his flesh and blood, a man of culture, an esthete of the highest caliber, receptive to the language of nature, equipped with fine hearing and an almost inexhaustible capacity for the assimilation of the emotions of the human soul and its expressions in painting, music and above all in poetry, a born 'naturalist' as he calls himself in one of his letters."

As indicated above, 1994, the centennial of Miskotte's birth, was celebrated in the Netherlands with symposia and lectures. The greatness of this man, as pastor, theologian, a cognoscente of culture, and as a human being, is increasingly being appreciated. He is still being read avidly and studied diligently, in spite of the fact that he is at times hard to fathom.[44] One hopes that his contribution to the theological renewal of the church in the face of progressive secularization and growing nihilism will continue to make its mark in spite of the obstacle of language.

2

On the Sources of His Thought

WHILE REFERENCE WAS MADE TO MISKOTTE'S EDUCATION AND TO his major works in the preceding chapter, this chapter will take a closer look at the possible sources of his thought, in the context of his intellectual development. Since the publication of his diaries,[1] we are able to gain a much more complete understanding of the sources of Miskotte's thought. This point should not be pressed, however, for there are many lacunae, which means that we are still forced to speculate.[2]

In the preceding chapter, several personalities have passed in review, any or all of which may have influenced Miskotte. We may also get a clue from his occasional lists of his favorite works in his diaries. On February 13, 1918, he included a dozen or so titles, among them: Friedrich D. E. Schleiermacher (1768–1834), *Der christliche Glaube,* St. Augustine (354–430), *Confessions,* and Johannes Hermanus Gunning Jr., Dutch theologian (1829–1905),[3] *Lijden en Heerlijkheid, Blikken in de Openbaring* [Suffering and Glory, Visions of Revelation] (1866), and *Leven van Jezus* [Life of Jesus].

On October 27, 1918, he wrote two more lists. The first were "books to be accepted because they express the human personality perfectly": Goethe, *Faust,* Shakespeare's sonnets, and Shelley's *Hymn to Intellectual Beauty.* On the same day he also listed some works "which shake the conscience": Leo Tolstoy (1828–1910), *Le salut est en vous,* and again, Gunning, *Lijden en Heerlijkheid* (which he read many times), Henriëtte Roland Holst, *Thomas More,* and the Gospel of John. However, unless one were to make a detailed study both of these works as well as of all of Miskotte's writings, it is quite impossible to assess exact influences, except to suggest the obvious fact that he was indeed a very well-read man.

Miskotte would not wish to label himself a biblical scholar, though his work witnesses that he knew how to practice "close reading."[4]

On November 15, 1918, he posed a number of questions about Scripture (in his diary), the fourth and last one being: "How do my heart and understanding relate to the Scriptures?" His answer: "Though educated under the Scripture as God's Word, the very deep things in my soul come from elsewhere." As noted in chapter 1, the bulk of his library consisted of non-theological books. His Zeitspiegel ("A Mirror of Our Times," the introduction to *When the Gods are Silent*) offers a brilliant analysis of non-Christian thought of the period, with his comments.[5] On December 16, 1918, he listed a number of what he considered the figures who influenced him most significantly:

Philosophers: Plato, Spinoza, Kant, Hegel;
Mystics: Plotinus, Augustine, Eckhardt, Böhme;
"*Poets (artists)*": Sophocles, Dante, Michelangelo, Shakespeare, Rembrandt, Bach, Shelley, Goethe, Beethoven, Hebbel, Mahler, van Gogh, and Dostoyevsky;
"*Community-creating heroes*": Luther, William the Silent, Bismarck.

The list seems to keep on expanding. It is difficult to draw any significant conclusions from this fact except the obvious one that his reading reflected his very broad interests.[6]

Dissertation Topic

Another indication of his searching without early tangible results was his period of uncertainty about what should be the topic of his dissertation. On January 8, 1919, he wrote down the following possibilities:

a. Significance of "Immanence" in Christian theology;
b. Sacrifice in religion;
c. The theology of Johannes Hermanus Gunning;[7]
d. Neo-Calvinism;[8]
e. Church and Art (the concept of culture);[9]
f. Religion and History (the concept of revelation);
g. Conceptual value of theodicy;
h. Philosophy of the History of Dogma.

As it turned out it would take him several additional years to settle on a topic, but it was not chosen from the above list.

Devotional Life

Miskotte, well-read in many fields, including philosophy, on rare occasions gives us a glimpse of what made him tick: "I am most profoundly moved, have experienced God the most realistically, and obtained the most useful insights, not from philosophical literature, only now and then from [Guido] Gezelle[10] and more rarely still with Tagore and van Eden, but most profoundly by the so-called devotional literature."[11]

This might suggest a mentality bordering on the pietistic, though he might strenuously deny this. But again and again he gives indications of the "softer side" of his faith. In his entry of Friday, June 13, 1919, he records that he spent a half a week in 't Boschhuis, to attend a "Pentecost Conference" of the "Brotherhood in Christ" which he describes as "a delightful revelation of the Christ life; I lost myself miraculously. Beyond all theoretical objections there rushed the stream of the single sentiment. Reconciliation with God and reconciliation with man were absorbed in one spirit of perfect love." The fact that two of his most favored authors were H. F. Kohlbrügge and H. J. Gunning (as indicated in chapter 1) may point, at least in part, in a similar (pietistical/mystical) direction. On February 12, 1919, he wrote: ". . . my deepest being is ethical—mystical-personal and only the mystical humanism of Goethe and Schiller well up in my heart."

Given the complexity of his thinking, his multiplied intellectual stimuli, and his deep religious feeling, it should occasion no surprise that his younger years were a time of frustration. We are reminded of the great St. Augustine, who took a long time to "find himself" and to discover his true calling in life.

On the surface it may seem quite amazing that Miskotte would become so keenly interested in the Hebrew Bible, for he certainly did not have, as far as we can gather, a very inspiring teacher in that field. His description of A. H. Edelkoort (1890–1956) is hardly flattering.[12] We have already discussed that in his university training his inspiration came not so much from his teachers, but from elsewhere; when all is said and done, it would be fairer to say that

Miskotte was intellectually "a self-made man." But his faith kept his interest anchored in the Hebrew Bible, and his calling faithful to church ministry.

His mental anxiety took a long time to resolve. On March 14, 1927 (when he was thirty-two years old) he wrote: "No one knows what a difficult time I am having. Sometimes I think that I can't possibly become old." On New Year's Day, 1929, he wrote some eloquent words about Scripture study, which would many years later be "fleshed out" in *When the Gods are Silent:* "There is hardly a word in our popular devotional (literature) and in our western theological language that truly has roots in the thought-world of Scripture. . . . (Scriptural) concepts which do not occur [include]: spirit, soul, conscience, as isolated substances or functions. Providence, guilt, the hereafter, truth, essence, supranatural . . . Instead, [we need] particular emphasis on: man, heart, flesh, the *acts* of God."[13] Here is an early indication of his insistence that theology and Scripture should form a creative alliance.

On March 2, 1930, he spoke of "the city as a castle of modern paganism. Self recognition: we are all pagans; and cannot be anything else. . . ." These words, also, would be developed more fully in his later works. Paganism was a major topic of interest for him, which is discussed at length in *Edda en Thora* and *When the Gods are Silent.*

Influence of Karl Barth

To the extent that Miskotte was indeed a "self-made man," this was no doubt due to his voracious reading, which has been repeatedly referred to. Not only did he read much, he grasped meanings quickly and synthesized what he had been exposed to. Prof. H. H. Miskotte, his son, has written that he thought that his father read with great concentration and quickly. A case in point: the volumes of the *Kirchliche Dogmatik* by Karl Barth: "When another hefty tome [of Barth's dogmatics] came out, he would withdraw with this 'catch' perhaps a day and half a night, during which time he would have gone through it thoroughly."[14]

Though Miskotte was preeminently a man of letters, in Karl Barth (1886–1968) he could enjoy both the man and his books. No person influenced him more than the Basel theologian; Miskotte considered himself a disciple. His diary entry of February 1, 1923, notes his comments on first receiving a copy of Barth's *Römerbrief.* He mentions its "ugly black binding, German script, yellow paper; the style seems expressionist, the thought Marcionite." But two days later he read Barth on Rom. 8:25ff. "Terrific!" He concluded that the *Römerbrief* both aggravated and fascinated him "by its shocking courage to relativize all values." On Sunday, February 4, 1923, after leading an extra service away from his parish, he read the *Römerbrief* until 3 A.M. and wrote: "Is the historical Christ needed? Does not the word suffice? After all, the incarnate Christ is promise again. Is the eschaton the abolition of time?"

A thorough study on the relationship between Miskotte and Barth is found in the dissertation by Jan Muis, *Openbaring en Interpretatie*[15] on whom some of the following comments rely. We may begin with the general comment that Miskotte is widely regarded as the theologian who introduced Barth to the Dutch-speaking world.[16] Miskotte experienced Barth's *Kirchliche Dogmatik* as a sermon, leading to love for Christ.[17] Muis comments: "Getting acquainted with Barth got him started as theologian and pastor; he was 'born again to the office.'"[18]

But Muis also discusses different nuances. For Barth, in true preaching God speaks. God has spoken and will speak in his Son Jesus Christ. For Miskotte: "God, who is nameless to the degree, that no definition can be given of him than what he himself has given in his *acts*, in his "act-words" [daad-woorden] and "word-acts" [woord-daden]: 'I will be what I will be. . . .'" Barth admitted that his own teaching had been put in an entirely new light.[19]

Unlike Barth, who would claim Christ (the Word) to be the axis around which theology centers, Miskotte, sticking closer to the biblical data, focuses on "the Name" (preferably with all caps, just as we write the tetragrammaton: YHWH). In *When the Gods are Silent* he discusses "the Name" in the context of his polemics against religion, "the one great concern of godless man."[20] Miskotte did not necessarily see a contradiction between the "Word" and the "Name." However, he would say that the concentration on Christ remains unintelligible as long as we do not understand the import of the Name.[21]

Muis does not see a contradiction between the two theologians.[22] While Barth follows a more or less logical/causal train of thought,[23] Miskotte often works phenomenologically[24] (particularly in two of his major works: *Edda en Thora, Wezen der Joodse Religie,* and in his *Bijbels ABC*). Also, the focus in Miskotte's work as a whole is on (German) Paganism, Modern Judaism, and Christianity. Muis writes that they "are highlighted in succession because writing and reading is a diachronic process, to be seen simultaneously in their context and unity. Miskotte is more interested in showing than in proving."[25]

Student of Culture

Miskotte's major works are all set in their cultural context; that is preeminently the case with *Edda en Thora* where it occupies virtually the entire book (his Auseinandersetzung with German Nazism), but also in *When the Gods are Silent,* which opens with its Zeitspiegel cum theological reflection. Unlike Barth, who interprets his themes theologically, Miskotte not only tends to describe some phenomenologically but also from a human perspective, highlighting personal, spiritual needs.[26] This is perhaps one of the most telling aspects of his literary signature.[27]

When we take an overview of Miskotte's works (apart from his four major books), we see that an important part of it consists of sermons,[28] meditations, and Bible studies.[29] In addition to these, he published studies of culture and Judaism. But when all is said and done, the insistent focus of his works aimed at preaching and instruction, suggesting that he remained faithful to his calling to the pastoral ministry—although he must have seemed out of place in some of his pastoral charges (in Cortgene certainly, in Meppel particularly, and to a lesser degree in his first Amsterdam assignment). It may be surprising that his Leiden professorate was not as happy a period for him[30] as was his pastorate in Haarlem and his later years in Amsterdam-South, where he worked with alienated intellectuals. His magnum opus, *When the Gods are Silent,* the last of his major works, was written as a practical book dealing with the question of how the Old Testament should be preached.[31]

3
Church and Synagogue

AN UNDERSTANDABLE REACTION TO THIS SUBJECT MAY PROMPT THE question as to why it should be needed for an exposition of Miskotte's thought on the Old Testament. It is, however, unquestionably fundamental for an appreciation of his theology. For one thing, Miskotte's world was Christian, flanked by paganism on the one hand (in his own time, not only the progressive secularization of the West [see his "Zeitspiegel" in *When the Gods are Silent*] but also virilent German Nazism) and on the other hand by Judaism. It is quite impossible to speak intelligibly about Miskotte's view of the Old Testament without an understanding of his relationship to Judaism.[1]

The Dissertation

As we have seen, when Miskotte during his student days cast about for a dissertation topic, Judaism was not among his options then. Clearly, during the thirties (most of which time he served in the Haarlem parish) he became increasingly interested in Judaism. That decade was also a time of escalating intellectual productivity for him, when he wrote two of his three (or four) major works: one on Judaism (*Wezen der Joodse Religie*) the other on German paganism (*Edda en Thora*).[2] When he finally wrote his dissertation in 1932 (*Wezen der Joodse Religie*)[3] he mentions the impetus that led to his choice was his reading of one of his favorite theologians, Hermann Friedrich Kohlbrügge (Dutch Reformed Pastor, Elberfeld, Germany).[4]

1. Judaism vis-à-vis Christianity

Miskotte mentions that the context for stating that Judaism must be treated as an independent religion is the far-reaching estrangement between Jewish and Christian spiritual life. "Not the national religion of a foreign tribe which would be irrelevant to us as Christians and Europeans came into view, but a balanced spiritual life, and a religious self-consciousness that felt itself called to do missions, rather than being the subject of missions, the self-consciousness of the elect."[5] We need to recognize and accept the Jewish, Talmudic pretention to continue authentically the Old Testament. "Should the synagogue not have the right to consider itself the rightful heir of the Old Testament and its history for the direct continuation of the history of the chosen people? Cannot the Talmud claim with as much right as the New Testament, to be recognized as the true complement of Israel's holy scripture?"[6]

With these (quoted) words Miskotte served notice that he would depart from the common Christian pattern of "dialogue" with Judaism that so often was (and is) motivated by conversionist goals, and just as often resembles a "benign anti-Semitism"[7] at best, and at its worst, a training school for pogroms and expulsions.[8]

Though the focus of the present study is the Hebrew Bible (which Jews call Tanakh or Miqrā', and Christians Old Testament[9]), Miskotte's reflections on Judaism color his view of the Old Testament and "stamp his entire theology."[10] Indeed, it seems that all of his works are to a greater or lesser degree "in dialogue" with Judaism[11] as they are, to a lesser degree, with paganism.[12]

2. Selected Jewish Theologians

Miskotte opens the body of his dissertation with a discussion of two thinkers who do not claim to have a "system" (of thought): Max Brod (1884–1968) and Leo Baeck (1873–1956). The major part of his work, which he labels "Systematic Foundation" (chaps. 2–4), gives expositions of three major Jewish theologians: the "rationalist" Hermann Cohen (1842–1918), Martin Buber (1878–1965) the "mystic," and Franz Rosenzweig (1886–1929), "existentialist." After a brief overview, two more sections follow. First, "Extremes" (chap. 5): Ernst Bloch (1885–1977), Constantin Brunner (d. 1937), and Franz Kafka (1893–1924), "in whom apocalyptic . . . 'atheistic' mysticism, and the problematic of Job are revived."[13] Then follows "Limits" (chap. 6), a kind of "counterweight" (figures of the new Jewish orthodoxy): Samson Raphael Hirsch (1808–1888), Salomon Ludwig Steinheim (1789–1866), and Hans Joachim Schoeps (1909-).

3. The Doctrine of Correlation

One of the key concepts to which Miskotte devotes much attention in his dissertation and which he also criticized is correlation.[14] In the teaching of Hermann Cohen, Judaism was based on the correlation of God's "being" with man's "becoming," leading toward the Messianic unity of humanity,[15] or, to state it somewhat differently, on the correlation of a holy (=moral) God with man being sanctified.[16] Biblical lyric, according to Cohen, may be understood as the speech of correlation; there runs a straight line from the Psalter to Goethe's *Prometheus*.[17]

God is not an idea, but pure being: "I am that I am." The world is becoming. The wide gulf existing between God and man can only be bridged by correlation.[18] In Christianity God is humbled in the birth and the crucifixion, but man is raised to divinity.[19] Sanctification, which Cohen calls an eternal process, is the essence of Jewish religion. In Cohen's teaching, which has been to a degree taken over by other Jewish thinkers, correlation colors the sum of human ethical, commandment-driven activity. Miskotte comments on how moral inactivity and fatalism annoy the Jewish spirit.[20] But he also speaks of the polarity of "holy adventure" versus "security, in people, family, and love life." Both security and adventure are aimed at sanctification.[21]

4. Critique of "Correlation"

The teaching of correlation, which Miskotte sees as a leading motif in his study, is also the target of his extended criticism since he believes that this teaching diminishes God and aggrandizes man. He writes: "The urge toward personifying spiritual actions and relationships is insatiable."[22] Correlation is seen as reciprocal sanctification. God as well as the people are thought of as "becoming." "This indecisiveness can only be maintained, because the anthropomorphic covers cosmic reality, because Jewish thinking transforms substances into functions."[23]

In his critique of correlation in the final chapters (7 and 8), Miskotte claims that there is no polarity in God himself. He is simple [eenvoudig],[24] his being is not determined by anything else. Secondly, "there is no correlation between the being of God and man, God and the believer, God and people. . . . God is never dependent on his creation."[25] Thirdly, "there is no correlation between divine and human acts. . . . The human act is one of obedience vis-à-vis the sovereign majesty, not an act which creates community between God and man."[26]

This is hardly the sum and substance of the argument of *Wezen der Joodse Religie*, but it should suffice to show that though Miskotte does his utmost to give a sympathetic exposition of Judaism, he felt free to offer his critique candidly and lucidly (as he did, of course, of Christianity). However, while he rejects the Jewish understanding of the divine-human relationship, he repeatedly expresses the dialogical "I-Thou" relationship which exists between God and man.[27]

Other Works on Judaism

1. Judaism Questions Christianity

In "The Question of Judaism"[28] Miskotte restates certain concerns which he raised before, namely, the questions which Israel asks of the church. While paganism accepts the world as it is and simply celebrates it, Judaism asks questions. These questions come out of the same intellectual milieu discussed above, namely "correlation." Judaism believes that man needs to participate in God's purposes. "[The coming of] Eternity must be accelerated [beschleunigt], it must be able to come at any time: 'today'; that is what eternity signifies. If there is no power, no prayer can hasten the coming of the Kingdom, then *so kommt es nicht in Ewigkeit, sondern—in Ewigkeit nicht.*"[29]

Judaism also engages in dialogue with Christianity about the meaning of faith. The question concerns whether μετανοια is a faithful translation of tešûbah.[30] Jews further wonder why God cannot forgive by himself and why he does not accept penitence except based on the sacrifice of the mediator.[31] Another fundamental question concerns redemption, and whether we can say in any sense that it has come. Miskotte cites these questions to help the reader realize some sources of possible confusion because of the different perspectives Judaism and Christianity offer, so that Christians may be aware of what a Jewish agenda vis-à-vis Christianity might look like.

In the sub-section "Opponent and Partner" Miskotte refers to the ambiguous relationship between Jew and Christian. The Jewish rejection of the Messiah is a negative factor. Nevertheless, Judaism has always viewed Christianity as "the way of the nations." Miskotte cites Yehudah ha-Levi (1086–1141) in *The Kuzari:*[32] "Those nations are . . . preparing for the Messiah for whom we wait, who will be the fruit, and all will acknowledge his fruit and him, and the tree will be one. Then they will praise and honor the root, which they once despised, as Isaiah says."[33]

Miskotte further brings into play the historical vicissitudes of Jews and how Jewish-Christian relations were affected by them. With a terrible holocaust in our relatively recent past, he sees a turn toward what begins to look like a rapprochement between the two religions.[34] Part of this is the renewed interest on the part of Jewish thinkers in Jesus and even Paul.[35] Miskotte hastens to caution that this does not mean that Jews have "come around" to the fundamental Christian affirmations about Jesus the Messiah. Yet, he believes the new situation to provide reassuring signs that both Israel and the church are not religions, but "live their life under the Word."[36] For Miskotte, the best hope for any sort of a relationship approximating reconciliation is if both Judaism and Christianity would listen to the Word, and honor the Name.

In the next subsection, "The Glory and Shame of Christendom," Miskotte draws some important conclusions from the dialogue between Judaism and Christianity. The glory of the church, such as her impressive growth must be seen as "a series of happy accidents promoted by favourable sociological circumstances."[37]

Theologically considered, it is due to the activity of the Word, but the church's progress has been vitiated by her ignoring Israel and being "disgraced by anti-Semitism." On the other side of the fence, "Israel's rejection of the Messiah accompanies the church like a continuing shadow." Even Franz Rosenzweig, though highly respected among Christian readers, declares that, yes, we crucified Christ and, believe me, would do it again at any time.[38]

Miskotte's voice, believing that Jew and Gentile stand under the same divine judgment, confronts both Jews and Christians and is therefore worth hearing. Jews have departed from the Old Testament, he claims; they live "in a pride which draws its strength from a 'religious' misunderstanding of the election, a 'correlative' understanding of the covenant."[39]

And Christians? They claim to have replaced Israel as the people of

God;[40] they have tutored the Gentiles in the ways of anti-Semitism.[41] Surprisingly, Miskotte does not mention the putative anti-Semitism of the gospels (for which certainly a case may be made), but he refers to Christian preaching which often supports military violence and obedience to ungodly governments. Finally, he points to the danger of focusing on the New Testament by itself, while ignoring that it constantly presupposes the Old Testament. He particularly refers to the Pauline teaching of Gentiles having been grafted onto the ancient tree. Gentiles are admonished not to boast, Paul wrote, since they do not "bear" (βασταζω) the root, instead, the root "bears" them (Rom 11:18).[42] Miskotte exclaims: "What is all the confusion in the history of doctrine . . . compared to this twofold burden which has been put upon the progress of the Word of God: the absence and deviation of Israel on the one hand and the usurpatory presence and unreceptiveness of the church on the other?"[43] Yet, in the midst of this situation, the church needs the vision of faith, and an open heart to perceive the mysterious works of God.

2. The Proposed Dutch Reformed Confession

When a proof of a new confession for the Dutch Reformed Church was published (ca. 1950), Miskotte wrote a commentary on its nineteen articles. It comes as close to a dogmatic as Miskotte ever wrote. The articles which concern us are chapters 3 ("The Election of Israel") and 17 ("Present and Future of Israel").[44] The attention paid to Israel (vis-à-vis the church) is quite remarkable, but it is probably a commentary on the different theological climate in Europe in general, and the Netherlands in particular which Miskotte had an important share in shaping. It is doubtful whether Miskotte, whose writing does not enjoy a reputation for universal clarity,[45] has ever achieved greater lucidity than in this book. He is consciously speaking to the church.

a. The Election of Israel[46]

At the outset of his exposition of the article on the election of Israel, Miskotte admits that there is a new element here.[47] He ascribes this to three causes:

a) a more historical understanding of revelation;
b) the new orientation suggested by recent events; and

c) a clearer insight in the secret of Israel's election, which Miskotte interprets as pars pro toto, representative, and as an example and pledge.[48] He blames the influence of anti-Semitism for our forgetting certain accents, such as the fact that "God meets us in *history,* that history is a weaving of grace and judgment, that the elect bear the heaviest burden in this world, which is still made heavier when they forget their own election; that what *happens to us* individually and what *is experienced* collectively, spiritually and physically—that in the midst of, and in spite of catastrophic estrangements, God remains faithful to his people."[49] At the same time, Miskotte cautions against an overemphasis on history, for "we do not live out of history, but out of the Word."[50]

God's kingship and man's rebellion lead to the confession of Israel's election. Miskotte skirts the "correlation" idea by stressing that God's relation to man continues; he does not abandon the work of his hands[51] as we see in Israel. But the election of Jesus Christ[52] precedes Israel's election, which is "but an image and application of the election of Jesus Christ and his body (the church)."[53] This means that the historical (horizontal) dimension must not ignore the vertical dimension of eternity and divine decision.

Since the draft-confession presupposes human apostasy (in the biblical record), Miskotte suggests that it may be labeled infralapsarian.[54] This is supported by the fact that Abraham seems to appear from nowhere. The covenant came about by divine initiative "that it might be *bilaterial,* a living relationship of spirit and spirit, heart and heart, act of God and human act, word and answer."[55] From the covenant relationship we also learn the divine attributes.

Here we meet again a motif that is of great significance with Miskotte, and it keeps turning up repeatedly: the movement from the *particular* (concrete) to the *general* (essence). The special destiny of Israel and her particularity points to the destiny of all of mankind as object of divine grace. "Man as such, who is estranged from his origin, is morally neither good nor bad; he is wrong [verkeerd], he has made a wrong turn [ver-keerd] but he does not repent; such is man! But God *turns* to him, God chooses him."[56] God's electing is that of a just and gracious king. His election is related directly to Israel, and indirectly to human destiny. It is specified as a "priestly kingdom and a holy people" (see 1 Pet. 2:5). It is therefore related to a people, a multitude, to the "supra-individual." Moreover, the destiny promised in election is not salvation but holiness, which is to be understood in a biblical sense: thus, it refers to a relationship which is dedicated to God. Miskotte goes so far as to say that "election *itself* is being-preoccupied with becoming holy."[57] "Election *leads* directly to *ethics*, it is being privileged to holiness. . . . Israel is chosen that it might realize that *salvation* [heil] and *peace* for mankind is found by living by God's royal favor and law." Favor comes first; the law is a gift of grace. "We live not so much 'according to' the law, but rather *by* the law, by the 'Torah,' the teaching, that directs our steps on the way."[58] Here Miskotte introduces not only a key motif of Reformed theology; he has also given his readers an insight as to how he views the relationship between Israel and the church.

Striking another familiar Reformed motif, Miskotte discussed the prophetic, priestly, and royal offices which he describes as characteristic of man's destiny. Though these functions are attested historically, they are now seen as describing man's nature as "holy." God himself is present in these "functions." In the course of his discussion, Miskotte again criticizes the Jewish doctrine of correlation: "Israel has not understood this being together with God, this paradise in the midst of all adventures, as *grace*. It has itself wanted to be a creating *partner;* it has wanted to use God to become pious and great; and finally it preferred to be alone and excused from the 'burden' of its election; it wanted to be like other people in all respects, and nevertheless to be apart and maintain the pretense to keep the name of 'God's people.'"[59]

He immediately turns to the relevance of his discussion of the church since we need to confess our solidarity with Israel's guilt: "About *you* this story is told." As a counterweight to his accusation against Israel's errors, he erupts with a moving, eloquent prayer of confession:

> We are horrible to look at in our bewilderment; pathetic in our loneliness; disgusting in our pretense, yet, in spite of all, "holy," different from the "world" and the "heathen," unintelligible in our unbelief. By confessing the election of Israel, the church pronounces the severest judgment on itself, on the immense hypocrisy, that goes with all human piety, on the unbridled tyranny which is joined to all human morality, on the hardness of its heart, the stiffness of its neck, the lovelessness of its behavior, the

despicability of its religious egoism; the lack of its apostolic fervor, the failure, it seems, of everything, of everything that we touch.[60]

He squarely faces the question as to why the church needs this article, which is, after all, a new departure in confessional statements. His answer is that we come to our faith not by way of philosophy, but via the Old Testament. Thus, Israel is like a mirror in which Christians see their own recalcitrance. Over against that stands the unchangeable resolve of God which spells salvation for the whole world.

b. The Present and the Future of Israel

In Article 17 of the draft confession ("The Present and Future of Israel"), Miskotte begins by saying that this subject has been widely discussed: "With Israel's martyrdom and its resurrection, with its exemplariness and its persistence, its biblical and religious impertinence, we have sympathized somewhat, fascinated as we are by this people, this church, this antichurch, and finally a sign of more-than-the-church, namely the sign and pledge of the Kingdom."[61]

Though some judge the church's increased preoccupation with Israel an aberration of sorts, to Miskotte it is more to the point to consider it the missing link in the history of dogma. In fact, Miskotte contends, if Christian theology had been more concerned with Israel, the unity of the church, which depends on thinking biblically-Israelitically, might be closer now. To American ears Miskotte may be, and often is shocking. Speaking about conversion, he suggests that it is *Christendom* which needs conversion;[62] for a start, Christianity should acknowledge the prime status of Israel as God's elect people, as well as the permanent relationship between God and his people.

Miskotte then begins to draw comparisons between Israel and the church. Israel has certain advantages, in that it is "biologically bonded in a common blood" while the church is composed of "the called out." Accordingly, the church's cohesiveness is weaker than the synagogue's, just as "baptism as a sign is paler than circumcision."[63]

The biggest problem in the church vis-à-vis Israel is the notion that Israel is finished, that the church has inherited the promises extended to Israel. We are reminded of older editions of the Bible where "curses" (oracles of judgment) in the prophetic books were said to be addressed to Israel, and "blessings" (promise oracles) to the church. Presently, the church seems to have encouraged Israel being frozen in a *galut* [exile, dispora] mentality, which is often satisfied with a natural knowledge of God, a distant memory of a covenant, and a faint reflection of Christian motifs. A halfhearted mysticism sometimes overwhelms history. Miskotte concludes: "It is shocking how little the [Christian] congregation carries on its heart in a priestly way the care of . . . the need of Israel before the face of God."[64]

Miskotte has (again) landed squarely in the area of Pauline concerns discussed in Romans 9–11. First off, he wishes to distinguish between the goal (τελος) of the individual and the people on the one hand, and on the other hand the temporary rejection motif which is a passing phase in God's dealing with Israel. If the latter is ignored, history, instead of labeling it "to be continued," will (rightly) be seen as "the conclusion." This would, however, militate against the divine promise, for as Paul affirms: "the gifts and the calling of God are irrevocable." (Rom. 11:29).[65] Miskotte finds that God's ongoing concern with Israel may be seen in two ways: (a) in the conversion of some to Christ (which creates vexation in Jews, leading to hatred for Christ), and (b) in the continued existence of Israel as a people (which is an offense to pagans, igniting anti-Semitism). Unwittingly, both Jews and pagans are joined in a rising aversion to the Word made flesh. In a sense, says Miskotte, the pagan reaction is more innocent than the Jewish response from whose midst the Messiah came. However, the draft statement affirms that Israel remains the people of the promise and the people of the Messiah: "Whoever is offended by this, is offended by God's sovereign dealings, to which he himself owes salvation. Whoever assaults them, assaults God's good pleasure and will not escape his judgment."[66] As an aside to Roman Catholicism, Miskotte charges that church with failure to recognize a lack of catholicity—because Israel is lacking! "Being 'outside' we must not be driven to the claim, that we are therefore the true Israel, whose history (church history) is really a second, higher history of salvation, with signs and wonders, sacrifices and saints, in gradual process toward glory, '*leaving Israel behind.*'"[67] In a historical aside, Miskotte believes that the Reformation (which he says is still young), when challenged to orient itself either on Rome or Israel, chose the latter.[68] Whatever Rome's decision (it has at long last recognized Israel!), "a re-formed [ge-re-form-eerde][69] church must know . . . that she has Israel beside her through the centuries, as a partner in expectation, as a teacher in biblical thinking,[70] as an admonition to humility, as a sign of God's judgment and patience."[71]

Miskotte next discusses divine judgment on Israel, referring to the notorious call: "His blood be on us and our children!" (Matt. 27:25). How often has this verse been cited in the Middle Ages as the prelude to (and an excuse for) a Good Friday riot (or even a pogrom!) where Jews' property or persons were attacked—supposedly in the name of Christ! Through the centuries this exclamation has functioned in this tragic manner. Robert H. Gundry comments: "To take v 25 as historical would require us to think that the people were claiming innocence. Composition by Matthew makes their words an acknowledgment of guilt."[72]

Conclusion

In an article on Buber, Miskotte wrote (in 1958) that Jewish-Christian relations have moved "in shocks." Before that, Christianity thought it could leave Israel and Israel's faith alone, unless it might be reduced to the ethical principles of the prophets (as they were then conceived). With the Sermon on the Mount in the New Testament, the two testaments were thought to make contact.[73] In the same article Miskotte credits Buber's literary-historical work with our improved vision of what binds and what divides Israel and the church. It has become clear that tolerance was often a cloak for indifference, it was an openmindedness between pagan Jews and pagan Christians. But that has changed for the better. "The present conversation takes place between true, faithful Jews and true, faithful Christians. The unity lies . . . in a different order, namely, in the manner of God's Covenant and Election." Unity can no longer be found in such ideas as a common belief in God, while excluding the question about Christ. Buber quotes Franz Werfel with approval: "What would Israel be without the church, and what would the church ever have been without Israel?"[74]

These comments, written for the common reader, epitomize something of Miskotte's reflected views about Judaism. He cannot very well be faulted for "having sold out" to Judaism. The remarkable thing about his dissertation, which was unique for that time, is that he could write objectively, "from within" as it were, yet offer thoughtful critique and maintain his Christianity. There is more to be said, however. In addition to his phenomenological and systematic approaches, Miskotte's work was also historically and culturally oriented. In a sense, that is the mainspring of his work, apart from the forceful biblical/theological thrust of his ministry. All of these aspects need to be borne in mind for an appreciation of his literary output.

When we lay Miskotte side by side with Barth, we notice immediately that Barth's orientation appears Christological, whereas Miskotte is concerned with the Name, revealed in the Scriptures (beginning and ending with the Old Testament!), to trace the acts of God. That is one of the reasons why Miskotte's work appears to bear a more Israelite stamp than Barth's.

Thus, while Miskotte rejects the Jewish idea of "correlation," he has nevertheless accepted certain aspects of it, as for example in his use of some of the "partner-with-God" language.[75] It might be difficult to find a Christian theologian who has made a more concerted attempt to stay close to the Old Testament while respecting Jewish categories insofar as they agree with biblical thought. Not surprisingly, he is very critical of Christians (and the Roman Catholic Church is particularly singled out for criticism; he wrote before the Second Vatican Council!) who live by the New Testament (alone), or who pay insufficient attention to the Old Testament, who might be said to be guilty of some kind of benign Marcionism. Undoubtedly, Miskotte's work may take some credit for the fact that the churches in the Netherlands as a whole pay far more attention to the Old Testament than churches in the United States.[76]

The discussion on Judaism was intended to show quite clearly that for Miskotte, the Old Testament is about Israel, about divine election, about the gracious purposes of God in the world. He took Romans 9–11 with complete seriousness as scholars are more apt to do in our time. As we have seen, it was still a problem for the Reformers, particularly for Luther. Even Barth's thinking on the relationship between Israel and the church, Miskotte felt, needed some changes.

In all, Miskotte, as pastor and teacher, had a passion for the Scriptures. Though he read many books, when he read the Scriptures, he knew himself to be addressed. In faithfulness to the Scriptures, he formulated Christian teaching in the best way he knew, marshaling his enormous gifts of head and heart with which he was blessed.

This is a good place to stop. The nuts and bolts of Miskotte's biblical teaching, as informed particularly by the Old Testament, are to be taken up in chapters 5 and 6.

4

Religion, Paganism, and Nihilism

THE CONCEPTS THAT MISKOTTE CONSTANTLY REFERS TO, AND against which he delimits [abgrenzt] his exposition of the biblical message, particularly the message of the Old Testament, are "religion," "heathenism" or "paganism," and "nihilism." The definition of these "systems" and how they function in theology is fundamental for understanding Miskotte.

In his *When the Gods are Silent,* Miskotte is concerned with a dialogue between "the fourth man,"[1] who is a modern representative of paganism, and the Hebrew Bible, the assumption being that, whereas the gods are silent, the God of the Old Testament speaks and wishes to communicate. In this, Miskotte follows Martin Buber and Karl Barth. Buber said: *"Meinen wir ein Buch? Wir meinen die Stimme."*[2] Barth wrote: "God's Word means that God speaks. Speaking is not a 'symbol' (as P. Tillich . . . thinks). [When we speak of God's Word] it means that 'God speaks,' and all else that is to be said about it must be regarded as exegesis. . . ."[3]

Religion

A major aspect of Miskotte's polemics is directed against what he terms "religion." Barth wrote: "We begin by stating that religion is unbelief. It is a concern, indeed, we must say that it is the one great concern, of godless man."[4] Thus, religion is seen as the chief obstacle to faith.[5] In fact, if Christianity is made into a "religion" it becomes as silent as the gods of paganism.[6]

Discussing "the Name," Miskotte paints an eloquent contrast between religion and faith:

> Religion signifies the experience and celebration of the cosmic equilibrium in a rite; faith relates to the Word. Religion has a strengthening

> effect upon the movements of the intellectual life, whereas faith is more likely to be disturbing. In every crisis of society religion functions as an ordering force; faith adds to it a disturbance which goes deeper than a crisis, namely, the creating, establishing, and ordering of a relationship. Religion clings to the mutual relationship of "God" and "man"; faith clings to the free, spontaneous "turning" of God to man. Religion issues in culture, is itself the foundation and pinnacle of culture; faith, cutting straight across the given existence, hears tidings of a breakthrough, an end, a fulfilment, which are beyond the grasp of all human action, which, in the full sense of the word, "overcome" man.[7]

Yet, he also discusses the possibility of a continuum, "a basic Christian and religious stock," the "Christian" quality of Western life. Christian reflexes are still noticeable in modern thought; he cites Spengler, Huizinga, Toynbee, Rauschning, and Eliot but points to the relativization that makes itself felt.[8]

In his section "Removing the Rubbish" (*When the Gods are Silent,* 61–65), Miskotte touches on the corrupting influence "religion" has had on the Old Testament, not appreciating the fact that the Old Testament, dynamic as it is, constantly surprises us. However, the common perception of the Bible often leads in the direction of "religion." Miskotte may exaggerate somewhat in his list of erroneous notions that he would label "religion" instead of "faith." Thus, he claims, "Providence" is often a circumlocution for "fate," and "fear of God" may be related to "guilt." "'Atonement' is a kind of fraud; the cross is 'a level bridge athwart the abyss of death for men who pay the bridge-toll' . . . Mortality is . . . punishment. . . ."[9] Such notions are only a step away from atheism; they do not need the "living God" who addresses men in his Word. In his chapter on "the Name" Miskotte faces the issue head-on. Fundamentally, he states with emphasis that the confession "YHWH is the Godhead" is irreversible, in spite of the fact that both Jewish and Christian theologians have claimed otherwise. The philosophical path on which such theologians embark, claims Miskotte, will inevitably be blocked by Ludwig Feuerbach who will label their attempts "disguised anthropology."[10] The one relates to being justified, the other to being sanctified.

Paganism

"Paganism" or "heathenism" is another one of Miskotte's labels. In fact, he often speaks of pagans, Jews, and Christians.[11] As a Christian theologian, his main interest is chiefly Christianity and its rootedness in Judaism as these two biblical faiths mutually strengthen each other. In fact, he claims that the unity of the Scriptures delimits paganism, setting the boundary between Christianity and paganism. Thus, at the risk of generalizing, we may say that Miskotte regards Israel's religion as anti-pagan, even if one may read things in the Old Testament which have a pagan ring. Muis claims that Miskotte's paganism is akin to Barth's religion, in that both confront revelation.[12]

How does Miskotte define paganism? He often refers to it by name in *When the Gods are Silent,* where we meet such comments like that "we are by nature all pagans."[13] He comes perhaps closest to a definition in *Edda en Thora* where he asserts that paganism is the religion of the human heart, always and everywhere,[14] not the same as atheism, liberalism, or libertarianism, but a constant ferment in human life.[15] Miskotte proposes to honor paganism, to look at it afresh.[16]

Jan Muis claims that Miskotte has concretized religion into paganism. Whereas according to Barth, revelation judges all human religion, Miskotte's phenomenological approach makes distinctions among religions.[17] In a sense, Miskotte's targeted audience in *When the Gods are Silent* is church people who are at risk making the move from "ungenuine" to "genuine nihilists." Thus, he is constantly pointing out the types of erroneous thinking which threaten to take them from being a "third man" to a "fourth man." This links up admirably with his counsel in *Edda en Thora* that Janeff's claim be taken to heart: "The old gods will indeed return, but with new faces. Only their power over man and their laughter over the sins of world history will be the same. They will be coming back, that is certain. The hour of their return will be the final hour of the Christian era."[18]

In *When the Gods are Silent,* during the aftermath of the Nazi era, Miskotte writes that the great majority of German youth recalled the gods to life,[19] but "this renascence of paganism appears now to have died away."[20] However, even in *When the Gods are Silent* he is not given to total optimism: paganism "with its numinous figures is always present," coming to the surface as "archetypes" from the unconscious.[21]

Miskotte laments that "we are constantly showing a lack of understanding, appreciation, and admiration of *paganism.*"[22] He is particularly concerned with common, initial reactions to the Old Testament, particularly in connection with our perceptions of God.[23] Here Miskotte juxtaposes such "standard" attributes, commonly found in theologies, such as omnipotence, omnipresence, and omniscience,[24] versus the biblical characteristics, which are signs of his love and his good pleasure; he mentions "grace and faithfulness, righteousness and mercy, retribution and forgiveness" and asserts that these are to take precedence over the former group mentioned, since they would isolate and hypostatize God, making YHWH into a silent God among the silent gods which would amount, for Miskotte, to a paganizing of Old Testament faith.[25] Thus, the lines are drawn: when the Word of God is heard and believed, paganism is curbed. This means that the church needs to remain faithful to her apostolic mission; if that does not happen she will fall "victim to the old powers, or . . . [harden] into a new institution of religion."[26] While paganism celebrates the status quo, and is satisfied with "what is," the Word of God confronts, challenges, and calls for change. In this, Christianity stands shoulder to shoulder with Judaism, which asks questions about the meaning of life.[27]

In his Bible study on Jonah 3, Miskotte discusses the motivation of the Ninevites, "pagans," who are under the grip of nature. "What motivates them is that one question, that leaven of enthralling uncertainty, of audacious expectation, which exists in the outstretched hands, the uplifted heads, and the hearts that reach out beyond all that is humanly conceivable (Rom. 8:19). They are driven by that one question in which a good unbelief begins to stir and a good belief begins to dawn: 'Who knows, God may yet repent and turn from his fierce anger. . . .'"[28]

Surely, the God who acts to extend his mercy is not the immutable God, but the God of the Scriptures (grudgingly confessed by Jonah, the rebellious prophet) who is "gracious and merciful, slow to anger, and abounding in steadfast love, and repenting of evil." (Jonah 4:2).

Nihilism

This is a subject that is particularly acute in Miskotte's *When the Gods are Silent.* A very helpful study is G. W. Neven's "Miskotte over 'God voor en na zijn dood' [Miskotte about 'God Before and After his death']."[29] According to Neven, Miskotte is the first Dutch post "death-of-God" theologian. His second point is that his encounter with Judaism played a decisive role in his theological development.[30] This is particularly evident in Part I of *When the Gods are Silent*, his "Kleine Zeitspiegel," in which Miskotte places nihilism center stage. There is a dynamic development in this part of the book. Beginning in Part I, Miskotte introduces his "fourth man" (1–7), whose world of "silent gods" (7–13) is systematically described as nihilism, differentiated in the "genuine" (14–19) and "ungenuine" varieties (19–24). Concluding that the gods are silent as they always were, and that modern man can no longer believe, Miskotte proceeds to take spiritual inventory. We are no longer pagans, but nihilists; neither "Being" nor "Word" carries any meaning. Neither subjectivism, nor the hint that there is "something" outside of me, is nihilism.[31] Nor are "autonomy of reason" or "feeling" part of the nihilist stance.[32] However, Miskotte discovers an Achilles heel in Nietzsche's criterion of pleasure and displeasure, which he describes as "a sympton of increasing despair because the hedonist and utilitarian, if they are ever touched deeply enough by their failure, are necessarily driven to pessimism."[33]

The only way out for Miskotte is the cancellation of the autonomy of the human mind. When driven to the wall, Miskotte can only suggest that the Scriptures be permitted to speak in their own categories, giving them precedence. Those who listen will hear its particularity, not its universalism; in other words, it takes a "lower road," moving away from the grand sweeping labels of yesterday's theology: instead of "omnipotence," the Scriptures speak of specific "saving acts"; instead of an "absolute God," of "the Name."

However, the greatest weakness of nihilism is its "ungenuine" mutation, which Miskotte calls "rebelling conformism," or "the reverse side of 'ungenuine' religion."[34] The perpetuation of "religion" and of "natural theology" insures the continuity of ungenuine nihilism.

According to Neven, in Miskotte's "system" as explicated in *When the Gods are Silent*, three concentric circles may be discerned:

a. Faith in God has become completely unobvious.

b. Effects of the culture shock of the "death of God" on personal life, the interpretation of tradition, and the dialogue with Judaism.

c. The experience of time as the theater in which not only the final decisions are made about life and death, but also in which the common life is celebrated as a daily recurring gift.[35]

In the shock of "the death of God" in personal life, in exegesis, and in the dialogue with Judaism, three lines may be distinguished:

a. A *biographical* line, which refers to Miskotte's description of the "fourth man" for whom neither God nor Jesus exist. Neven cites Miskotte's familiar quote from John 1:26: "See, he stands in your midst, one whom you do not know."[36] After the death of "Almighty God" the images of life, love, death, friendship unto death had to come from the depths, just as one notes that in John's gospel the death of Jesus leads to a new language.[37]

b. A *hermeneutical* line, i.e., the interpretation of Scripture for modern culture, by careful observation of biblical texts, even those texts the forms of which no longer speak to us, but make room for listening to God which sometimes leads to disappointment or aggravation. Since Miskotte's time, biblical scholars have been more generally convinced of the *Schönheit der Bibel.* Concomitant with that appreciation there has been increasing interest in letting the text have its say—a motif that Miskotte frequently refers to in *When the Gods are Silent.*[38]

c. The *dialogical* line, highlighted particularly in his dissertation (*Wezen der Joodse Religie*). Neven claims that in this, too, the concern is the transition from God "before" to God "after" his death. Just as for Rosenzweig Nietzsche was the one who triggered his search for redemption,[39] so Miskotte was inspired by the revival in Jewish thought in the late nineteenth and early twentieth centuries (which he describes in his dissertation), in contrast to Christianity which was in dire need of renewal.[40]

This is where we must stop the discussion on nihilism. That we should next turn to the Old Testament is in deliberate imitation of Miskotte's *When the Gods are Silent* where his "Kleine Zeitspiegel" is succeeded by "Zeugnis und Interpretation"—of the Old Testament that is, for according to Miskotte, in the Hebrew Bible man may encounter "the Name." Explaining this, he writes a sensitive essay on Simone Weil, French Jewish writer, who had rejected Judaism but never quite came to Christianity, though she made many statements that suggested her preoccupation with faith questions. Miskotte uses the metaphor of radioactivity, which had been left in the air since "the explosion of the Name"; in other words, Weil, though she tried hard to reject any and all faith, felt confronted by the God whom she kept rejecting. To her, God was an "insistent presence." She wrote: "We know nothing of God's essence, but we do know what he does to us."[41]

5

The Old Testament

THIS CHAPTER WILL FOCUS SPECIFICALLY ON HOW MISKOTTE DEALS with the Old Testament. Though in all of his writings the Old Testament is, if not the immediate subject, at least fundamentally involved, the study of Miskotte is difficult for a variety of reasons, some of which have already been hinted at. Professor Doberstein, the translator of *When the Gods are Silent,* has elaborated on this point. Helmut Gollwitzer's review of this work in the October, 1963, issue of *Evangelische Theologie,* refers to the difficulty of his style, being not always perspicuous. "The obscurity which has often been attributed to him is apparent in many parts of this book in so far as the logical sequence from sentence to sentence is often not immediately discernible and sentences are frequently loaded with all the associated ideas in the author's mind."[1] Neither is this complaint limited to those who do not know Dutch. Muis speaks of his "sometimes tiresome phrasing."[2] Additionally, his magnum opus, *When the Gods are Silent,* which has been seen as containing his system in its most complete form, undertakes a great deal indeed: beginning with its Zeitspiegel, mixed with theological reflection, it discusses modern Judaism, Germanic paganism, all against the background of his interpretation of the Old Testament. His exceedingly fertile mind, his unbelievable control of the literature, his ability to penetrate the writings he tackled, and his enormous skill at synthesizing his material all contribute to the difficulty of fruitfully studying his works.

This section presents an overview of some of Miskotte's salient points on the Old Testament. First, something of a historical overview of his critique of Old Testament interpretation will be offered. Though he never claimed to be a biblical scholar, his profound interest in Scripture study is evident. In "Unity of Scripture" something is said about how he viewed the relationship between the testaments. This is crucial, for Miskotte has been charged with conceding too much to Judaism, as in effect relegating the New Testament to an inferior position. The next section deals with the "surplus" of the Old Testament over the New. This refers to various Old Testament themes which the New Testament does not take up or continue. They have receded into the background.[3] Miskotte is more concerned with the surplus than with the deficit because he is convinced that precisely these themes have communicative (kerygmatic!) potential for nihilists.

Six of them have been selected (out of a list of twenty) for discussion, beginning with the "primitive mentality," which for Miskotte, far from being a liability, describes authentic biblical thinking, or, as he calls it, a "getting away from the spell of religion."[4] In the next item, "acts (or deeds) of God," man is confronted by concrete events with a definite purpose, for this is how God reveals himself. "The Name," which logically should have followed, will be discussed in Chapter 7. "Narrative" is a record of the telling, an account of "holy history," of God's dealings with Israel. It is Torah, i.e., teaching. The "names of God" (in addition to "the Name") do not add anything to the full meaning of God as God, but, as Miskotte put it, they have nevertheless enriched and intensified the Name. The metaphor of color might illustrate. An object itself is not changed by the addition of color in our representation of it, but in terms of human perception, the addition communicates something significant. Next, on the fringe of God's world, and often troubling man, are the powers (which are also mentioned in the New Testament, and in that sense somewhat less suitable as a candidate for a "surplus" aspect). Finally, "eros" is selected from a range of items dealing with human life. Taken together, this selection of themes should suffice to illustrate what Miskotte intended to convey by his term "surplus." Highlighting them is another way in which he affirmed the unity of Scripture in a world where nihilism is rampant;[5] he is convinced that the Old Testament has much to say here.

It is not difficult to find references to the Old Testament in Miskotte's work. The most logical place to start is his best-known work, *When the Gods are Silent,* which is brimming with references to the Hebrew Bible. Thoughtful readers quickly discover that Miskotte has many refreshing things to say. That is quite useful, since Old Testament scholars have all too often become technicians, who consider it quite meritorious to read and interpret the biblical text with an absolute minimum of theology. That is something one could hardly accuse Miskotte of! He would heartily endorse the dictum, one suspects, that theology is the queen of the sciences. For him, the Old Testament is *the book* (the Scriptures!) of the synagogue and the church. As a Christian, he is adamantly opposed to limiting a practical canon to the New Testament and the Psalms, for the New Testament must be seen Israelitically as well as the Old.

Accordingly, the reader will immediately notice his use of certain labels which may seem novel or unfamiliar. Fundamental to this is his advocacy of the Jewish order of books, i.e., the division into three parts of Tôrāh, Nĕbîʾîm, and Kĕtûbîm, which is the basis for the acronym TNK=Tanak, instead of the common (Alexandrian) order followed by Christian Bibles.[6]

In *When the Gods are Silent* we discover why Miskotte spends so much time and energy on the Hebrew Bible. Modern ecclesiastical lingo might call this an evangelistic agenda: he is concerned with communicating with the unchurched, not only with the representatives of "the fourth man" but at least as much with the "third man" who is also in danger of embracing nihilism. In fact, he shuttles back and forth between these modern representatives of paganism and the Bible in his Kleine Zeitspiegel while in Part II ("Witness and Interpretation") he turns to the Old Testament in earnest, which, he says, contains "the very healing and saving power the 'fourth man' needs."[7]

Critique of Old Testament Interpretations

Before giving an exposition of Miskotte's constructive views of the Old Testament, it may be useful first to turn to his critique of misinterpretations, approaching the subject in the spirit of a via negativa. Generally speaking, Miskotte laments the church's misuse of the Old Testament (already referred to in the section on Judaism and Christianity, Chapter 3). By the second century C. E. the church had forgotten that *her God was the God of Israel;* the God of Israel became "an outcast for his newly won people."[8] During the Middle Ages the church became smug; Miskotte's critique of Roman Catholicism (regarding the Old Testament as a collection of Semitic stories, while admonishing the faithful not to spurn allegorization) is quite dated (Miskotte wrote in 1956!), particularly in view of Roman

Catholic developments since Vatican II.[9] However, the Reformation does not get excused either. Calvinists, especially Anglo-Saxons, are said to have interpreted the Old Testament literally. Yet, within the Protestant family, responses differed markedly, as becomes clear when one compares for example Reformed with Anabaptists.[10]

In his chapter "Removing the Rubbish" (61–65), Miskotte catalogues several misunderstandings. But the Old Testament can cure them all: ". . . where it is allowed to act and speak for itself even a little, it sets up a happy carnage among the articulated misunderstandings which are typical of 'religion' and therefore the typical lodging places of the 'ungenuine' nihilists."[11]

What does Miskotte mean by "rubbish"? He enumerates a few telling examples of what he considers gross misunderstandings of what the Hebrew Bible tries to communicate: providence misunderstood as "fate," the fear of God as "guilt," love as an "emotion," the neighbor as "everybody," creation as "formation," atonement as a "fraud," and mortality as "punishment."[12] He may be stretching the point, but it is hard to deny that he is touching a sensitive nerve in the theological thinking of not only people in pews, but even of preachers in pulpits. This is related to his repeated insistence that the affirmation "God is love" may not be turned around: "Love is God."[13] God is greater than the sum of all the "attributes" which we may ascribe to him. Miskotte is convinced that only if the Old Testament is read properly, such false notions will be discarded and then healing can commence. He likewise condemns philosophical constructs which illustrate the metaphysical understanding of God and the world, and which the church has accepted, such as: the ontological cosmos, natural law, providence, amor fati, the result of which is the dimming of "the light of the God of Israel."[14] On the popular side, the Old Testament is appealed to for practically anything: polygamy, nationalist hate, racial pride, as well as their opposites.[15]

Though he is sympathetic in his treatment of Judaism (cf. his dissertation!), he does not give Judaism "a blank check" anymore than he does Christianity, especially in regard to its attitude toward the Bible. He cites the fact that in Orthodox circles, Talmud study has often overshadowed interest in the Tanak.[16]

In his *Bijbels ABC* (to be referred to in greater detail in chap. 6), Miskotte urges his readers on to a new reading of the Scriptures, not a falling back to a kind of atavism, like the colloquia pietatis, or conventicles, or the spirit of former generations which were, claims Miskotte, "Bible-strict" [bijbelvast] but not "faithful to the Bible" [bijbelgetrouw]: there are those who appeal to the Bible and quote from it, but they may not necessarily represent the meaning of the text.[17]

One sometimes gets the impression that Miskotte emphasizes the Old Testament at the expense of the New, as if the proclamation of Christ in both testaments is set aside. Muis thinks that this is not the case. "For us, non-Jews, it is Christ who by closing the history witnessed to in the Old Testament, opens the text of the Old Testament for us as proclamation and teaching."[18]

Miskotte's influence moved well beyond the discipline of theology in its narrow sense. He is also considered a major inspiration behind the so-called Amsterdam School (of exegesis and interpretation).[19] In the ongoing conflict between philosophies of translation: on the one hand, the dynamic-equivalent mode (like the American *Good News Bible),* on the other hand, *concordant* methods such as Buber and Rosenzweig[20] or *idiolect* translation (the Amsterdam School). Miskotte stresses the importance of etymological roots[21] as well as context. Without such attention "every translation becomes superficial, information in the style of: 'This is what it boils down to.'" (49)

The Unity of Scripture

In spite of Miskotte's high regard for the Old Testament, he affirms the unity of the Old and New Testaments. He bases this first of all on their textual and spiritual unity (beyond their historical continuity), but also in their unified witness.[22] He parts company with the Christological interpretation of the Old Testament and speaks of the "fatal idea" which holds that the New Testament is revelation and the Old Testament *preparation* for that revelation.[23]

Miskotte also criticizes an all-too-confident assertion of the unity of the testaments. The reason, he says, is that it tended to reduce the meaning of texts to an idea, a truth, or a doctrine. More apropos is his own observation that our encounter with God in Scripture is more apt to take place via the esthetic or the imaginative, than with rational concepts or philosophical ideas.[24] He is not hesitant about ascribing credit to those who have aided our appreciation of the artistic quality of the biblical literature. He mentions Hamann, Herder, Boech, Dilthey, von Hügel, and Rudolf Otto.[25]

Miskotte expresses the unity of Scripture thus: "*Before* and *after* the coming of the Son, the life of man depends on the *encounter* with the God who sent the Christ. At the same time, this order becomes clear to us: *first the Old, then the New Testament, and finally the Old Testament again.* For the encounters before and after are encounters with the same God, YHWH."[26]

Earlier, in his dissertation, he touched on the same subject. The kerygma of Jesus the Christ, the crucified Lord, whose death ushered in the coming of the Kingdom does not mean the cancellation [Entwertung] of the Old Testament. "To the contrary, the kerygmatic content of the New Testament Scriptures which do not present themselves as Word of God, is borne throughout by the authority of the only valid Word of God . . . the Old Testament. . . ."[27]

He writes in the same vein in *When the Gods are Silent* where he criticizes the attempt to read Christ into the Old Testament. "The process is rather the reverse; we need constantly to be learning from the Old Testament what is the content, the meaning, and the intent of that which we call 'Christ.'"[28] He would even go so far as to say that everything is in the Old Testament—including the New Testament![29] Surely, we may find foreign influences in the New Testament, such as mystery religions and apocalyptic. The Nazis tried to persuade Christians that the Bible was an Aryan, not a Jewish book, but, writes Miskotte, the gospel understood that there was nothing "foreign" (outside of the Old Testament) in the church's teaching. "That the content of this message [of the New Testament] is a different one from Moses and the prophets does not exclude that it moves in representations, words, longings, and certainty which come from nowhere else than the language of the Old Testament. . . ."[30]

Berkhof, who succeeded Miskotte in Leiden, has called attention to the differences concerning Scriptural unity between Barth and Miskotte. He has expressed it this way: The Word of God comes in three "forms" [gestalten]:[31]

1) the Word become flesh in Christ;
2) the written Word in the Bible; and
3) the proclaimed Word in the church.

With Barth, the second and third form are determined by the first. But with Miskotte the first hides behind the second according to

Berkhof.[32] Muis expresses this point in a somewhat more nuanced manner. He writes: "The heart of Barth's doctrine of revelation is: God has expressed himself fully in the man Jesus Christ; this Son is the Word of God and this Word of God is God himself. . . . When Miskotte speaks about the Word, the notion of Word as address dominates. By speaking, God directs himself to man and establishes fellowship with him."[33]

Barth's approach is Christological from the outset: "The Old Testament covenant is the revelation of God as thus specially defined, in so far as, being so defined, it is expectation of the revelation of Jesus Christ."[34] As mentioned at the beginning of this section, for Miskotte the unity of Scripture lies in the Name, revealed to us in the form [Gestalt]: אהיה אשר אהיה (Exod. 3:14), as he writes in *Bijbels ABC:* "The Name has its roots in one divine Name. This name is a secret sign which we cannot fathom. It is the name YHWH . . . best translated as 'I will be with you, as I will be with you.'"[35]

Miskotte has been called a "theologian of the Word." A fundamental aspect of his theology is the unity of Scripture (in its two components, the Old and the New Testaments). As we have seen, he reverses the traditional order which tries to find the New Testament in the Old. Instead, he begins with the Old Testament, and ends with it as well. Miskotte's phenomenological approach (particularly in his *Bijbels ABC*) demonstrates his conviction of the unity of Scripture. More so than with Barth, for him revelation and Scripture are close together.[36] The Word made flesh, God's self-revelation in Christ, is primary for Barth, though he insists that whether the Word is understood as revelation, Bible, or proclamation, it is one and the same Word.[37] The Bible is the manner in which the church remembers past divine revelation, and expects future revelation. Thus, the major focus is on revelation; the biblical witness points beyond itself, it is derivative. The Christ event remains primary. Miskotte is keenly involved with the hermeneutic of the Bible in a world in which nihilism is a constant threat. More than with Barth, Miskotte emphasizes the present life,[38] human experience, which anticipates the Word of God.[39]

The Surplus

On the subject of the relationship between the Old and New Testament, Barth and Miskotte clearly differ. Barth held that neither Testament can be understood by itself, since they speak in different ways about the same revelation and the same God. This becomes apparent with certain themes shared by both testaments, such as: covenant, God's hiddenness, suffering, guilt and judgment, and hope. The New Testament presupposes this basic structure, with the only difference that in Christ is fulfilled what the Old Testament anticipates. In a sermon, Barth has called the Old Testament one great prayer, the answer to which is found in the New Testament.[40] Clearly, Barth's theology is Christological throughout.

1. Definition

Miskotte proceeds quite independently from his master. Muis laments that Miskotte speaks too briefly about the "deficit" of the Old Testament, compared to the "surplus" (Überschuss or Zuviel or Rest).[41] The meaning of these concepts is simply that if the two testaments are placed, one on top of the other, one shows up with material the other lacks. It turns out that Miskotte found a sizable number of elements that constitute the "margin" of the Old Testament surplus over the New. But he quickly adds that he is most concerned with elements which are particularly relevant for the present world. The New Testament does not surpass or deny them; rather, they are receding into the background. Miskotte, who is constantly concerned with proclamation, believes that these "surplus" elements are precisely the kind of material that may be helpful in communicating with nihilists. Some themes which Miskotte labels "surplus" will be discussed next.

2. Primitive Mentality

The first aspect of "the surplus" (chapter 3, Part II of *When the Gods are Silent*, 173–302) is entitled "The Primitive Mentality."[42] The bibliography Miskotte cites provides a clue to the topic: Pedersen's *Israel*,[43] Buber and Rosenzweig's *Die Schrift und ihre Verdeutschung*,[44] Thorlief Boman's *Hebrew Thought Compared With Greek*,[45] A. R. Johnson, *The One and the Many*,[46] G. van der Leeuw, *Religion in Essence and Manifestation*.[47] These references are cited here not only to suggest that Miskotte was fully abreast of the best and most recent literature (*When the Gods are Silent* was first published in 1956!), but also that he had absorbed the respective thrusts of these works. He closes this section as follows: ". . . the Old Testament serves us as a testimony of the one revelation, the one covenant, the one incarnation, the one presence of God on earth. . . ."[48]

3. The Acts of God

The principle we have met several times, namely, "from the particular to the universal" is also in evidence in Miskotte's exposition of the "surplus" of the Old Testament, as for example in his section "The Deeds of Yahweh."[49] Miskotte attacks "rationalistic" theology where God-talk is reasoned out in detail. Terms such as "omnipotence" are anathema with him.[50] Rather, he begins with the smallest building block, the specific words by which God is introduced to the world, such as: maʿăśeh, mĕlāʾkāh, ʿabōdāh, all of which mean "act" or "work." God is distinguished from the world by his (specific) acts, which all spell love. The key to Miskotte's thought here is: "From God's deeds there grows the knowledge of his 'virtues' and in the knowledge of his virtues his nature."[51] He then quotes a formula (a liturgical doxology), elements of which recur often in the Old Testament: "YHWH, YHWH, a God merciful and gracious, slow to anger, and abounding in steadfast love and faithfulness, keeping steadfast love for thousands, forgiving iniquity and transgression and sin. . . ." (See Exod. 34:6f; Num. 14:18; Ps. 103:8; 86:15; 145:8; Neh. 9:17; Jonah 4:2.)

4. Narrative

If God may be known from his acts, how are those acts to be distinguished from other events? To that question Miskotte answers: by listening to the Word. He refers to Isa. 55:11 which describes that Word as powerful, "magical"(!), evocative, dynamic, effectual. Here also Miskotte stays very close to the Hebrew text, keeping in mind the Hebrew vocable dābār which remains ambiguous in Western languages, which must choose between "word" and "thing." This leads him to coin the phrases "deed-word" and "word-deed."[52] He warns, however, that the continuity of history is hidden. The acts of God are remembered "in a uniquely appropriate kind of narration in which a special way of remembering is actualized." Such narrative is (derivative) Word, as distinguished from the "act-word" of God himself. It is Torah, i.e., instruction. No hidden meaning or moral are to be gleaned from it. Neither are we to look for the precise historical kernel or original experience of the persons involved in the narrative. Miskotte exclaims: “What [a] pity it is that we have been so long accustomed and are still inclined to think of the narrative as a mere vestment of some higher content! And what a pity that later Judaism thought of it as an illustration of the Law and extended this conception to the whole of the Scriptures!”[53]

What is now commonplace, Miskotte already wrote in 1945, namely that the Bible is essentially a story that is shared by retelling. As it is being retold, the hearer may discover who the God of the Bible is. To tell a story well means that the center, beginning, and end of everything becomes visible—parts of the one Presence, pure act, love. Involved in all of this is truth, which in the Old Testament means neither a pure object of knowledge nor a pure encounter with being. “Truth is the act of God through which unfathomable human existence is drawn into the history which is at once his history and ours. Our past is his, his future is ours. His hand was in our past, our future is participation in his ultimate and penultimate acts.”[54]

5. The Names of God

Miskotte puts a great deal of emphasis on the significance of the Name. Undoubtedly, he learned from Orthodox Judaism which calls God haššem: “the Name.” That is certainly preferable to the (French) Jerusalem Bible which uses l’Éternel, or even to Buber in his famed translation: ER.

Miskotte urges the necessity of nuancing “the Name.” He rightly points out that the Old Testament has other names for God beside YHWH: Elohim, El Shaddai, YHWH ṣĕbāʾôt [the Lord of hosts] and others. Again, a warning is sounded against reversing name and predicate. Saying: “God is love” is not the same as: “Love is God.” God and the epithet are not to be exchanged.[55]

6. The Powers

Miskotte makes a connection between our concept of the powers and primitive speech. The powers are not the essence of life, they are marginal. The Name in which life is grounded constantly meets this limit. This fact is repeatedly expressed in the lament prayers in the Psalter. The psychological awareness of these "supercreatures" is noted particularly by youth. Miskotte (quoting O. Noordmans) calls it a "cosmic dizziness, a fear of existing without God."[56]

Miskotte warns that any speech about the powers should be related to the Word. The Old Testament, however, speaks mythologically, and in passing as it were. It seems surprising that we are told in the creation story that God created the *tanninim* and in Ps. 74:13, 14 that their heads are broken. Whatever the precise meaning may be, Miskotte asserts that this is the way God made the world, making it habitable though constantly threatened, so that it needs to be defended and protected.[57]

Another "power" of which similar things may be said, is death and šĕʾôl [the grave]. The difference is that it is more urgent and personal. All of this has pastoral ramifications for Miskotte, who claims that the fact that we live in the real world—the world of death, of the powers—is often repressed: "Much Christian preaching hangs in the air because it refuses to admit that there are dark experiences even for faith and precisely for faith. When we no longer face the powers that walk without shape or form within and around us, the liberating power of the gospel tends to turn from a miracle of God and become an axiom of religiosity."[58]

As we hear of Jesus' exorcisms of demons in the gospels, we learn that the powers may be exorcized through Christ and his Spirit. In the gospels, and knowledgeable exorcists know this, excorcism is accomplished by the Name. Miskotte calls this the perfect autocracy of the divine Presence. Yet, as in Jesus' ministries as recorded in the gospels, these are not trials of strength. If they were, why did Jesus not exorcise all demons of his contemporaries and heal all the sick of ancient Palestine? Though the dominion of God is hidden, it is not arbitrary. That is the word we hear in Exod. 33:19 and there is no recourse from that word: ". . . I will be gracious to whom I will be gracious, and will show mercy on whom I will show mercy."[59]

7. Eros

Miskotte rightly refers to two New Testament references which, if taken by themselves, would lead to anxiety and confusion: the admonition that "those who have wives live as though they had none" (1 Cor. 7:29) and the new order of the Kingdom, which says that there will be no more marrying, but those who are called will be like angels of God (Matt. 22:30). It is unacceptable for Miskotte to suppose that the New Testament thinks ascetically, since the Old Testament does not. In the Old Testament, marriage serves propagation. Genesis 2 and the Song of Songs consider the man-wife relationship very positively. Jeremiah 2 and Ezekiel 16 use marital metaphors to illustrate the covenant relationship between YHWH and Israel. These four references constitute the Old Testament "surplus." Miskotte gives a remarkable and sensitive discussion on the subject in the section "Eros"[60] with particular attention to the canonization of the Canticles. He simply affirms what has now become a common view, namely that allegorization or spiritualization are inappropriate interpretations. He quotes Rosenzweig with approval: "Only the love of the lover is this constantly repeated self-giving; only he gives himself in love. The beloved receives the gift; it is this, the fact that she *receives* it, that is her gift in return, but in receiving she remains with herself, and becomes a completely passive and blessed soul."[61] Love that increases to the point of constant faithfulness, that is the love illustrated. Miskotte cites Rosenzweig's exclamation: "This is how God loves!" and concludes: "Truly, the mystery is 'great,' incalculable, very near in order that we may touch it, too far for us to be able to embrace it, since it rather embraces us in our innermost being."[62]

Exegesis

In his article entitled "Exegesis" in *When the Gods are Silent*, Miskotte labels the term "theological exegesis" a pleonasm. This is a relevant comment in exegetical scholarship as well as a reminder that we are dealing with the book of the church. Moreover, exegesis is not a method of reading, but rather "a fruit of reading" by which Miskotte seems to mean reading as encounter with the God who reveals himself. He does not seem interested in "hyphenated theology" as a companion of exegesis and repeatedly insists that the Bible needs to be allowed to speak for itself.[63] Related to that is the point that, in the Old Testament, the Masoretic Text is the text to be exegeted.[64] What some have called a "vicious circle" [circulus vitiosus] is for Miskotte a "circle of truth" [circulus veritatis], that is to say, theology has its own logic.[65]

Muis, who has researched the relationship between Barth and Miskotte, indicates topics in Miskotte which are lacking in Barth; among them are:

1) *Language.* On this subject, Miskotte learned from Buber and Rosenzweig: language is both address and answer.[66] Grammar is compared to a lit-up mirror reflecting the structure and movement of true life.

2) *Life,* as Muis correctly points out, is a favorite word of Miskotte's.[67] In his study on Job, Miskotte joins "word" and "life":[68] "Because God addresses us, we are persuaded with primary force and originality that we live; that is how we truly know what life is."[69]

As to Scripture itself, Miskotte claims that it has become completely man's word. With Barth, he does not claim that there is a need for any special biblical hermeneutics. Scripture wants to address man, or rather, God has a communicative intention through the words of Scripture. In *When the Gods are Silent,* Miskotte gives the sequence of the receiving of revelation as follows:

1) first, the word as *sign,* as a pointer to pay attention,
2) next, the intended matter, or the *content* of the message,
3) and finally, the word in terms of its *intention.*[70]

Miskotte never hesitated to accept the "assured results" of modern biblical criticism, though he did not feel hidebound by them. In *Levende Woord,* when he discusses exegesis, he explains the relationship between literary-historical, phenomenological, and theological exegesis, using the terms *looking* [kijken], *seeing* [zien], and *hearing* [horen]. These three mutually influence one another though not necessarily in that order. Theological exegesis is engaged to interpret and apply the Scriptures, without acknowledging dogmatic systems or philosophical presuppositions.[71]

Miskotte begins, however, with what he terms "literary-historical exegesis": the "looking," which he describes as a human, scientific activity, to be engaged in freely and without hesitation. Still, this should not be interpreted as granting a secret hegemony to this approach. While recognizing that the Word of God has become human, it must be given the right of way, to say what it (he!) has to say.[72] Miskotte is particularly emphatic on this point, which he reiterates a number of times in *When the Gods are Silent:* "There is a series of themes which are common to both the Old and the New Testament, but which occupy a broader place in the Old Testament, so that in order to do justice to the unity of the Testaments in preaching and instruction we must at these points go back to the Old Testament, which as it gives its independent witness, *demands that it be allowed to speak 'for itself. . . .'*"[73]

Miskotte is fully aware of the secularism of literary criticism: "it is profane, through and through" and it is risky to recognize its methods.[74] But, says he, theology itself is likewise a science [wetenschap]. Exegetes cannot afford to ignore what scholarship has done before.[75] However, with Barth, he did not excuse the prejudices of critical scholarship: the Word, as in Scripture, comes to us in human form.[76]

The "seeing" aspect of exegesis is likewise necessary since the exegete is bound to the text. Understanding refers to what is *written* [geschreven], not what is *described* [beschreven] and the latter must be made subservient to the former. Since it is impossible to reconstruct the factual occurrence of revelation, the structure of the writer's thought, and his view of the events, the biblical metaphors all take on heightened significance for the understanding of the text. The "looking" and the "seeing" work both successively and beside each other. The sense precedes the words and is transcendent vis-à-vis the words, like the melody compared to the musical notes. Translating is an attempt to keep the melody with a different tonal system.[77]

In his *Bijbels ABC,* Miskotte writes in a less technical, more popular vein. Reminiscent of one of Karl Barth's sermons, "The Strange New World Within the Bible,"[78] Miskotte wrote as his introduction of *Bijbels ABC,* "De omgang met het boek [Contact with the Book],"[79] which speaks of the Bible that opens up like a world in itself, to live in, to live out of, to hide oneself in, to arm oneself.[80] Contact with Scripture occasions revelation:

> Then, when there is somewhere the first rustling of new life, an awakening, a rubbing of the eyes, a groping for firmness, a joyful recognition of the half-seen and half-confessed, when there is an experience of the pain or pure regret over lost time and wasted opportunities and when those first signs of life move straight through all denominations [richtingen] and bring together people who formerly paid no attention to each other, when the inertness is shot through with new intentions—that comes from nowhere else than the presentiment, the suspicion of the presence of truth.[81]

In addition to John 1:16 he cites Deut. 30:11, about the commandment that is said to be not too far away and not too hard. This is a pastor speaking, describing how the Word comes alive with people. The danger, writes Miskotte, is that we may lapse into some sort of piety, when people are "fixed on the Bible but not faithful to it." He warns against self-made religion, but urges starting with the Scriptures where authority resides (as opposed to our judgments).[82]

To gain understanding of what we read (Acts 8:30)—the underlying theme of the eleven chapters of his *Bijbels ABC* —we need to be taught the spiritual grammar, the basic outlines of Scripture. Thus: back to the ABCs, for Scripture's witness is directly opposed to paganism, our natural religion.[83]

In the fall of 1957 Miskotte gave four radio lectures on the subject "Biblical Hermeneutics," subsequently printed in the journal *In de Waagschaal*[84] (in 1958), then translated by Hinrich Stoevesandt (as he did many of Miskotte's works).[85]

He set the stage by commenting that since theology is humble, it does not offer space for invention and phantasy. As such, it does not have a speculative epistemology [Erkenntnisweg]. It is text-bound, i.e. to the text of the entire Bible in its unity and diversity, in its synthesis and opposition. This circumstance makes it very difficult to discover the unity of the Bible. Hermeneutics concerns itself with the art of interpretation [Dolmetschen]. "The concern is not so much the interpreting of a foreign language into one's own, or a complex word into one more lucid. Rather, the concern is the interpreting of one thought into another, which is intended to be the same, thus the relationship of a thought expressed in a certain manner to the truth intended. . . ."[86]

Miskotte mentions only Herder and Dilthey as milestones in the science of interpretation, but discusses Martin Luther in greater detail. He cites two passages: first, his defense when he was criticized for his translation of the New Testament,[87] where he laments that he, a single doer, has many masters. To balance this statement, he quotes Luther's famous statement, which he scribbled on a sheet of paper two days before his death:

> No one can understand the Bucolics and the Georgics by Vergil unless he has been a shepherd or a farmer for five years. No one can understand the Epistles of Cicero, unless he has responsibly occupied himself and been a statesman for twenty years. No one could think to have tasted

the Scriptures, unless he has led a congregation for a hundred years with the prophets. Therefore, mighty is the miracle: John the Baptist, Christ, the Apostle. Do not attempt to undertake the divine *Aeneid,* but bow deeply, adoring their tracks [vestigia]. Wir sein pettler. It is true.[88]

Miskotte duly notes Luther's humility in his description of the difficulty of the interpretation of Scripture, leading to the conclusion that it is never completed.[89] The verbs Luther uses are intelligere and gustare, which Miskotte understands existentially: "Exegesis is a work which cannot be done without participating in special, spiritual experiences, and at the same time a work which can only make itself intelligible, can only be made applicable through existential, summarizing basic words [Grundworte] for final structures."[90] Contrary to those who would seek their hermeneutical keys in mystical experience or history, Miskotte claims that Luther originated the approach he advocates: "Do not try to cross a sea, to undertake a journey through the world, stopping at every port, but bow yourself down and adore the vestigia, the tracks . . . along the road of truth."[91]

For Miskotte the tracks [vestigia] pertain to the matter to which the words relate: the tracks of the verbum Dei. "The vestigia are the precipitation [Niederschlag] of the promises of Christ and indicate the true meaning [verus sensus] which can lead to the true experience [verus usus]. Tracks, however, even if they are but footprints, have a form [Gestalt], in this case a word-form, in representation and concept. . . . 'Wir sein pettler' means . . . that the vestigia make us into beggars—beggars in spirit, and such beggars are called μακαριοι."[92] If God is to speak freely, man must get out of the way, except that he is invited to hear, that he might understand.

6
The Biblical ABCs

As Miskotte begins with his series of biblical "keywords," though he is writing to a wider public (and as the printing record suggests, in spite of the fact that this work is "dated" to a certain extent, it is still being read!), there are many touches of eloquence and elegance as well as many quotable quotes. Some of them are set forth in English translation here.

While Miskotte worked intensively with the Old Testament, he did so most obviously in *When the Gods are Silent* and *Bijbels ABC.* The difference in treatment is quite apparent. In the former, the concern is to let the Old Testament speak to the nihilist in his world where the gods have been silent. *Bijbels ABC,* on the other hand, offers a more phenomenologically oriented analysis of the Old Testament. These works have many topics in common, even though the Sitz im Leben differs: with the former it is modern, postwar society, where "the death of God" made its profound impact; the latter is a piece of "resistance literature" (from 1941!), an attempt to provide the most crucial elements of biblical grammar for the common reader. In this chapter, some of these elements are highlighted.[1]

The Word

In *When the Gods are Silent,* Miskotte ends the section "Eclipse of God" with a reference to Isa. 45:15: "Truly, you are a God who hides himself, O God of Israel, the Savior." In the section that follows, "The Word," he re-introduces the same verse and sounds a strong psychological note, claiming that the negativity of God's hiddenness is accompanied by a yearning for revelation. At some point this hiddenness is even perceived as an act of God: a potential bridge from the absent God to the God who reveals himself. Thus, God's hiddenness may serve an important preparatory function. To declare that God is in hiding, says Miskotte, is to make a confession of faith. His hiddenness is "full of happy promise," making a new beginning possible.[2] That beginning is, of course, his Word.

Considering the first two volumes of Karl Barth's *Kirchliche Dogmatik* (Church Dogmatics)—subtitled "The Doctrine of the Word of God"[3]—it appears that Barth and Miskotte speak the same language. On closer investigation, the differences become apparent. While Barth lays enormous stress on "the Word," Miskotte places great emphasis on "the Name," more than on "the Word." Muis, who wrote a thorough comparison between Barth and Miskotte claims that the essence of Barth's docrine of revelation is: "*God has revealed himself completely in the man Jesus Christ; this Son is the Word of God and this Word of God is God himself.*"[4] "Word" for Barth therefore signifies self-revelation. With Miskotte, however, the Word is primarily "address."

Since Miskotte wished to understand the Scriptures (which he calls a "witness of the Word")[5] *Israelitically* (as, in his view, Barth did also), he calls attention to the Hebrew vocable dābār. As Vriezen says, dābār is "far more dynamic and concrete than its Western equivalent, . . . it is a concrete, living matter. . . ."[6] Miskotte's explains: "*Dabar* is the sovereign event in which fact and meaning are one. It is the act which speaks and the word that intervenes. . . ."[7] In Gen. 1:3 we hear the first "spoken word" in the Hebrew Bible: a creative word: wayyō›mer ›ĕlōhîm yĕhî ›ôr! While the "calling" word (Gen. 12:1), the "judging" word (Acts 5:5), and the "healing" word (Matt. 8:9) need to be distinguished, their unity lies, says Miskotte, in the "creating" word.[8] He cites Jesus' word in Luke 4:21: "Today this Scripture has been fulfilled in your hearing." In, with, and under that Word, "like a one-sided greeting, an embrace not asked for, an unexpected blessing, a magic wonder."[9] Rejecting ontology, Miskotte wants to replace the sequence "being—truth—explanation" by: "living—word—proclamation"[10] and warns against a magic conception of the word which is common in the Oriental worldview; however, "the term 'word' is itself anthropomorphic (if one prefers, Oriental-magical). . . ."[11] In Israel, creative power is ascribed to God's word, which is not naked power but salvific. Following the consensus of Old Testament scholarship, Miskotte interprets the movement of the Old Testament from liberation (exodus out of Egypt) to creation:

"The Lord has spoken to man, to Abraham, to the prophets; and that has accomplished deliverance [heil], opened a kingdom of peace, sealed the meaning of a chosen life; *thence* the prophetic spirit must understand creation as born out of the same source: the Word. He has *said:* you are mine; from that I know, that he has also *said:* let there be light."[12]

Miskotte goes so far as to say that what makes us human is not that we are "rational living beings" but that we have the Word. "To him [humankind] language is given, the crown of creation, the gate to all spiritual communication, the window and lookout to daily and eternal fellowship."[13] Indeed, the Bible is brimming with speech; its actors (God being the primary one) are constantly talking. The P creation account shows that creation was accomplished both by speech and acts. In a sense, it illustrates what is true throughout the Bible: words and deeds are not rigidly separated (dābār!), they are interrelated, just as Miskotte claims about God whose essence is known by his acts.

Man speaks because he is addressed, he is answering God.[14] One of the descriptions of the goal for Christians in the apostolic writings is τελειος (Eph. 4 : 13, where it is used as an adjective: "mature [manhood]"). Miskotte often uses the Dutch word *mondig* (mond = mouth); it refers to being of age in the sense of being able to communicate rationally. His goal in writing *Bijbels ABC* as he expressed it, is to promote *mondigheid*, usually translated "maturity" but it means more than that; it implies the ability to communicate—from faith. We live in an interim period, a time of waiting, till all of creation becomes vocal. Miskotte hints at the consummation, the τελος, when all shall "know" the Lord (Jer. 31: 31–34), which includes effective, mutual communication. In the story of the boy Samuel, asleep in the temple, when God tried to communicate with him, the hearer/reader is told: "Now Samuel did not yet know YHWH, and the word of YHWH had not yet been revealed to him." (1 Sam. 3:7). The cardinal difference between biblical faith and paganism lies precisely in the word and in speech, whereas paganism finds its ultimate expression in the dance and its highest form in heroic silence living under fate.[15]

The word is also related to love. Revelation is the love of the lover, but the word (as answer: prayer, thanksgiving, praise) is the love of the beloved. The human word in that context is nothing but a Yes, an Amen, in answer to God's goodness.[16]

Miskotte discusses the decline of the human word.[17] The immediate context when he wrote (during the Nazi occupation) was the mangling and distorting of language by the German occupation through their sustained propaganda. He writes: "The estrangement of God, of this God, must bring about confusion of speech, lying, violence, exaggeration, and hollowing out in this one medium of the spirit: language."[18] As Miskotte pointed out, one of the ways to aid the appreciation of the word is to appreciate the importance of silence. Silence as a creative pause carries a potential in the common life; it is an interval of (or for) the Word, not to be confused with mysticism, but prayer or "walking with God."

In all of this, the teaching of Barth is in the background. Both in revelation and the Word, Barth emphasizes radical discontinuity. On the one hand, there is the Word of God and Scripture; on the other, hearing and understanding: the human response to divine revelation. Yet, there is also a dialectic at work: Scripture is totally man's word, and the hearing is totally God's work. No hermeneutical program can guarantee our hearing the Word of God.[19]

As Muis views it, Barth left a vacant space that needed to be filled. "For Miskotte Scripture is more than a human word which only from time to time, again and again, becomes Word of God. Scripture is an enduring form [gestalte] of that Word that may be experienced."[20]

Scripture creates a form of life which brings continuity in the hearing of the Word. This hangs together with Miskotte's stress on teaching which is needed in addition to proclamation: the בית מדרש (bêt midraš) is needed to promote understanding of the revelatory experience.[21]

The secret of the church is that something exceptional happens: the Word.[22] Scripture witnesses to it and people reflect on it. Scripture opens up as a world to remain in, to live out of, to keep oneself [bergen] and to arm oneself.[23] Though the church has often only perceived it in part, the Word is near (Deut. 30:11). The reaction that needs to be resisted is "pietistic activity or skilful debating." Instead, we need to recognize the authority of the revealer and his word, which is not forced on us but offered to us. The grammar of Scripture is perceived in our reading, as we learn its ABCs. Miskotte concludes by calling for simplicity, unity, and harmony; to achieve that, we need to understand the Scripture: this is the rationale for his exposition of the biblical ABCs in the first place.

The Name

While the Torah is a kind of prolegomenon to the biblical ABCs, Miskotte considers "the Name" the most important of all the "basic words" of the Old Testament. "The word 'Name' is as it were the aleph of the biblical ABCs, the first and decisive line in the pattern [tekening] of divine thought; it is the cornerstone in the building of the scriptural treasure of words, which has had a marvelous supportive capacity [draagkracht]."[24] This suggests that the chapter about the Torah is a kind of prolegomenon, a "doctrine of Scripture" as it were.

For Miskotte, biblical faith begins with the Name, not with the godhead; the movement of faith is always from the particular (the Name!) to the general, not vice versa.[25] For example, when one says that YHWH is good, he demonstrates goodness in his own way; we cannot say that goodness is an absolute, of which YHWH is a particular example. This is because, in Miskotte's view, paganism, or the religion of human nature, defines the terms that impinge on faith. This necessitates that the reader of the Bible needs to set aside what the words appear to mean (since they are pagan definitions). "The prophetic spirit in Israel has adjusted (or restructured) the words, images, and concepts, to give witness in human relationships of the wholly other Relationship which God has ordained between him and humankind."[26] The Name signifies revelation. Miskotte speaks of the divine name, the Other, "in the sense of revelation, disclosure, the sphere of power, the order of blessing, guidance."[27]

To appreciate Miskotte's understanding of "the Name" it may be useful to glance sideways at a phenomenologically oriented Old Testament theology for an overview. E. Jacob claims that the Old Testament use of "the name" is related to "the desire to procure some weakening of a too vivid anthropomorphism: thus in Exod. 23:19ff. the *shem Yahweh* is on the one hand Yahweh himself, and on the other his substitute in which he shows his reality and by which he is able to accompany the people without abandoning his transcendence."[28] Already in this statement we sense the difficulty of arriving at a precise definition or description. But Jacob's phenomenological path gives us some useful outlines which may help to clarify for us what Miskotte is driving at. In Deuteronomy, says Jacob, there is a movement toward the hypostatizing of the name of YHWH.[29] In the same vein von Rad speaks of "the assumption of a constant and almost material presence of the name at the shrine."[30]

The Psalms seem to strengthen this tendency. In Ps. 103 : 1, parallel calls to worship refer to YHWH (v. 1a), then to the name, actually "the name of his holiness [šem qodšô]," v. 1b. Thus "YHWH" and "the Name" are used as parallels. Here, and in countless other cases in the Psalter, YHWH and the Name appear together. Jacob concludes that in "the Name" we have a more effective manifestation of the totality of the divine presence than angel (mal'āk), face (pānîm) or glory (kābôd).[31]

Muis opens his discussion on "the Name" by saying that where Barth speaks of the Word of God, Miskotte, in line with the language of the Old Testament (as suggested earlier), uses the "name."[32] This is related to Miskotte's view of revelation. In the fundamental (archetypal) pericope of YHWH revealing himself to Moses in the desert (Exodus 3), Moses is first called by name (twice); then he is told through cirumlocution that this is a revelatory time and place (in the command to remove his shoes, because he is standing on holy ground: he is in God's place), then God reveals himself, first, by identifying himself as "the God of the fathers: Abraham, Isaac, and Jacob)"; only when Moses presses to know his name, he says: "'ehyeh 'ăšer 'ehyeh,'" which continues to puzzle scholars as to how it should be put in English.[33] Miskotte's claim "that a name is immediately given to God when he is met, points out that true religion does not originate with thought"[34] is hard to dispute.

Already in his younger years, Miskotte stressed "the name." In an essay on Abraham which he wrote while he was still a student, he concluded: "Thus God is revealed as God, thus his Name, that is his revelation, is glorified."[35] Miskotte's most useful, systematic exposition is found in his *Bijbels ABC*.[36] In the building of the scriptural treasure of words, "the Name" is the cornerstone," he writes.[37] As throughout his work, he is constantly writing against the background of, or rather, vis-à-vis, paganism and popular religion. The Name is inseparably connected to revelation, as in Exodus 3.

Another useful approach is offered in his opening words in *Edda en Thora* where he mentions science and its concern with the giving of names. A name signifies distinction, connection, arrangement, and the annexing of what is foreign.[38] In the same vein he writes: "The name *distinguishes* God *from other beings*, gods and demons."[39]

He points out that many names in the Old Testament express something of their being; Eve, the mother of life; Cain, the begotten; Seth the sprig [stek]; Jacob, the heel-lifter; Israel, the prince of God; Moses, the one drawn out of the waters of death. In this connection, name changes, both in the Old and New Testaments, are highly significant.

God is revelation; he is not nameless, or the "all." The First Commandment: "You shall have no other gods before me" (Exod. 20:3) has another side as well: it implies that those other gods exist, but they *are not* the ones [Ze zijn er wel, maar ze *zijn* het niet].[40] Thus, Miskotte is not arguing monotheism. The commandment does not deny the existence of other gods. A number of Old Testament passages are cited which specifically speak of other gods, concluding with 1 Cor. 8:5f.,[41] but everything leads to the confession: "This God is our God." This God is the only, the almighty, the omnipresent, etc.[42]

Another important point is that the Name signifies our avenue of approach to God. "With the name we may address, call on, swear an oath, influence, obtain power." Adherents of a living religion address God by name and believe that they are called by name.[43] He adds a brief excurcus on prayer, which has power, because of the Name. The praying person who seeks, finds, for he seeks a person who reveals himself.[44]

However, Miskotte is not satisfied with the simple equation of Name and Revelation. The context is crucial. Thus, speaking in the Name is done on the basis of revelation; praying in the Name is pleading on the basis of revelation.

In Chapter 4 of *Bijbels ABC,* "The Names of God," Miskotte asserts that "the Name" should be kept distinct from the names of God. The Name is rooted in a single name of God: YHWH, which Miskotte suggests we translate: "*I will be with you, as I will be with you*" (Exod. 3:14).[45] Thus, God himself has given himself to be known in the center of existence, and humans (Moses, Israel, the church) are called and chosen to name that name and to call out its existence. This is not by human initiative; the knowledge of God must be given to man. "It is given to him in connection with a meeting, a relationship, a 'covenant.' This divine name is the anti-pagan monument par excellence; it is the boundary mark where all philosophical exploitation ends."[46] The church confesses that God is a "human" God, who has become flesh. His revelation is directed to man and has entered the form [gestalte] of a man, "which is so much 'smaller' than the All, which appears to be 'only a man,' and who just in that form unmasks all inhuman, twisted projections and demons."[47]

The name of Jesus Christ is the fulfilment, affirmation, and the perpetuation of the single divine name of YHWH. Thus Christianity can never be a new religion; the New Covenant is the fulfilment of the Old, but as a writing it is a commentary on the Old Testament; and finally, "I will be with you, as I will be with you" underscores his free, "unlimited power" [vrijmacht] which is faithfulness itself: "See, I am with you always, to the end of the age." (Matt. 28:20). For Miskotte, the equation is: the Name=Revelation; the name=YHWH, the name=Jesus Christ.[48]

Prophecy

Prophecy is not one of the "words" in *Bijbels ABC* though it is discussed in *When the Gods are Silent.*[49] The first discussion is presented in the context of the "surplus" [Überschuss] of the Old Testament (discussed in chapter 5).

At the outset Miskotte insists that prophetism should be seen from within its Old Testament context. He makes little of the prophet as an ecstatic, stressing instead that the prophet is "spokesman of the concrete Word of God." Old Testament prophetism flowered in Christ. The Word is primary, and Miskotte will not hear of a definite (fixed?) teaching of the prophets. What is primary is the specific application of the prophetic Word to a given time. Only with such a definition is the freedom of God assured. Since the Word that the prophet receives is from God, the prophetic sphere is that of an office or a ministry. He is a servant of the Word, *verbi divini minister.* With approval Miskotte cites von Rad who claims that the prophet essentially says the same thing to everyone; "he only varies it according to the differing situations of those who receive his message."[50]

Miskotte's comments are targeted for "the third man" in the context of instruction; as such, they tend to be phenomenologically oriented (much as in *Bijbels ABC*). The prophet brings good news: "This Word is your life" (Deut. 32:47). The Sitz im Leben of the prophet's ministry is Israel's covenant life, as it relates to the given moment. In some of the prophetic books (in Jeremiah particularly) we see the severe consequences of faithfulness in the prophetic office. Had Miskotte seen Heschel's books on prophetism, and his discussion of the pathos of God, he most likely would have found himself in complete agreement.[51] As a result of his prophetic activity, the prophet becomes self-estranged (see the "Confessions of Jeremiah") which is, thus Miskotte, rooted in his surrender to God. "He is like God in the suddenness, the surprisingness of the encounter he initiates. He speaks in the name of God, and he utters grace and judgment with an authority that goes as far as functional self-identification with God."[52]

On the other hand, the prophet also lives in solidarity with the people of the covenant. He represents the God-given possibility within that people, as if he were a harbinger of a more favorable future for them. As such, the prophet critiques the society of which he is a part, pronouncing divine judgment on them. Miskotte singles out for criticism: "self-sufficient religion, the withering of the ethos, the institutionalizing of religious life so that it became merely automatic custom. . . ."[53]

Prophetism has had a pervasive influence on all of the Old Testament. Both the Torah and the Psalms are influenced by prophetism; this is of course a long way from claiming with Wellhausen that the prophets preceded "the law." Miskotte retains a balanced view in his comments on prophetism as representing the ethical triumph of the Kingdom of God, and on prophecy as prediction. He rightly opts for "concrete speech of God spoken in its [appropriate] situation. . . ."[54]

In prophetism also there is the movement from the particular to the general: from the specificity of Israel, the "particularity" of election, the "singularity" of the name, to the universal message, in anticipation of the Kingdom.[55] Miskotte, having heard some eloquent Jewish voices (such as those he discussed in his dissertation), is calling for the erection of signs of the Kingdom, signs of hope for a lost world: "We appear to be straining ourselves to the limit—while neglecting the obedience that must be rendered in witnessing precisely at the point where the world seems so sadly to have lost its way. We talk in many different keys about a 'fallen creation' (an entirely unwarrantable concept according to the standard of the Torah) and precisely in doing so we let mankind fall."[56] Finally, he laments about what he calls a "fatal flaw" in church dogmatics in that it hardly has room for prophetism. As far as Miskotte is concerned, dogmatics typically goes wrong from the outset; it proceeds from the absoluteness of God, tracing history back to creation, and interpreting redemption as restoration. "The prophets, however, spoke of creation only incidentally, suggesting it as a background, a threatre, a springboard; they saw no direct path from creation to fulfilment, but rather followed the wonderful road from the little deliverance of the little people of Israel through YHWH . . . to the final redemption and . . . the 'creation' of a new heaven and a new earth."[57] Once again, Miskotte has deliberately chosen to follow the lead of the Bible and its most competent interpreters.

In his article "Prophecy and History" Miskotte continues the subject. The Bible is God's history with man, and it is told from the standpoint of man. "He steps into our place. He comes to us and puts himself on our side. He tells us his history as our history."[58]

The Acts of God

Chapter 7 of *Bijbels ABC* discusses the "acts" (of God). Here again, as he often does, Miskotte emphasizes the need for letting the Bible have its say[59] even to the point that we might experience shock or bewilderment. The two extremes, between the "bloody reality" with stories which are all but edifying, to the pietistic sphere of Bible reading or the parlors of the rich and famous, may be avoided by stressing the unity of Scripture, in spite of its colorful variety, its wild reality, and the Tendenz and climax of God's acts. It is of the essence to know God "*as he has given himself to be known.*"[60]

God's acts determine our knowledge of his attributes. According to Wright: "God is thus known by what he has done."[61] Miskotte claims that his acts inform us of his attributes. He cites many examples, both from the Old and New Testament, to underscore his point. We have seen how he coins the word "deed-character" [daadkarakter] of revelation. However, not every historical event may be labeled as "act of God." If that were the case, spiritual life in the biblical sense would fade into religious respect for Providence, "then the spiritual judgment would be overcome by . . . brute fact, then praise would die in the congregation. If the telling, lauding, and praising of the acts of the Lord would not be *a being occupied respectfully with the particular*, the exceptional, then the entire liturgy, the entire worship is emptied of meaning."[62]

The central act of all of God's acts, the final and absolute is the sending of his Son, the coming of the Messiah, "the totality of his words, works and wonders, the act-of-all-acts, that is his death and his resurrection. There and only there we have to learn the character, the meaning, the purpose that is characteristic of all of God's acts, of all those acts which he has done *in* the world, *against* the world—and now we may add: finally *for* the world."[63]

Since the sending of the Son, human life depends on the *meeting* with the God who sent Christ. Thus (as indicated above), we move from the Old, to the New, and back to the Old Testament. Our meetings are with the same God, with YHWH. The unity of Scripture is related to the fact that the acts of God become meetings for us; thus, the teaching (Torah) is a world in which we may live: spiritual life, which is blessed by meetings, the acts of God whereby he meets us with his attributes.

The acts of God, qua particular deeds, become acts of world-historical and cosmic dimensions—but not because we begin with omnipotence or omniscience or such universal attributes, for creation, covenant, and the sending of the Messiah are particular acts.

The Attributes of God

This is, of course, not "a keyword," but rather about various adjectives describing God, the "wholly other." Human language can never describe God adequately. Miskotte intends to offer some caveats for the attentive reader. One is that the modifier must not "overgrow" the substantive, i.e., God; in other words, the adjective may not usurp the place of the Name, as in: "Goodness equals God."

Miskotte is also concerned about the proper order of the attributes, which are given for our benefit—for us who are by nature pagans. In part they are pleonastic, since the Name (of God) includes many attributes without our having to explicate them. Nevertheless, attention needs to be paid to the order for our sake. In contrast to the god of paganism, which is an unknown, the God of Israel and the church is the Name, the Lord with his Name, "and that Name is rich, an abundant world to live in; the holy . . . teaching leads us to that Name; that Name includes God's attributes and God's acts;

everything that is in the Bible spells for us that Name with the attributes and the acts."[64] He issues another fundamental caveat against wrong starting points:

1) If we begin with "infinity," we disturb the way of the knowledge of God's Name, canceling beforehand the reality of meeting;

2) If we begin with "omnipotence" and "omniscience" we also disturb the way of the knowledge of God's Name, for then we find no room for acts of mercy and justice;

3) If we begin with the equivalence of communicable attributes e.g. "justice" and "mercy," we dissect the Incarnation of Jesus Christ.[65]

Exod. 34:6,7 is cited to illustrate his point.[66] Miskotte denies that the writer could have put just as well: "YHWH, YHWH, *almighty, omniscient, omnipresent. . . .*" This would have swallowed up the attributes. Miskotte, rather than describing the supposed "essence" of God, prefers biblical, relational terms. Thus: "the omnipotence of the Lord is the power of mercy and grace, the power of patience and faithfulness, the power of forgiveness and reward; the 'infinity' is the qualitative preponderance of his mercy, his grace, his patience, his faithfulness, his reward, his forgiveness."[67]

This God is different from any and all gods and from anyone that is called god. Miskotte draws his application: "Praise is the gladness which has saturated the marrow of the soul, the gladness that we need not be pagans any longer, that we have been led out of the enclosed divine power of nature, the deification of the state, the 'black land': Egypt (Exod. 20:2), from the slave house of the demons, and that the holy teaching [Torah] continues to prevent that . . . the Lord himself again becomes an X and emptiness, a night and even a kind of devil."[68]

Instead of beginning with "omniscience" and "omnipresence," Miskotte prefers to begin at the other end, by saying that we can acknowledge that God knows something, that he is somewhere. Biblical language which speaks of God being in the Temple, in Christ, in the congregation, in the sacrament, does not exclude his universality. The so-called communicable attributes precede, while the incommunicable ones follow. When God is compared to an eagle (Deut. 32:11) that does not mean that he becomes an eagle, but that he (in some respect) acts like one, etc. Miskotte is quite emphatic on this point: "So-called systematic thinking, i.e., a thinking that would bring the revelation of God into a closed context, from a general concept, that is rooted in unenlightened thinking, destroys order, darkens our spirit, confuses our conscience, robs us of the joy of salvation, dampens among us the praise in the worship of the congregation, the silent ecstasies of the individual and the gratitude for the common life."[69]

Thus, in all of Scripture as holy instruction the way of our knowledge moves "*from the particular to the general*, from quality to quantity, from the moment to the view of the ages, from the particular Name to the divinity of God, from the special power, manifest in cross and resurrection, to the omnipotence over the world with an eye on the future, from the particular forms of the presence such as: the Temple, the Word, the Sacrament, to the omnipresence, from the particular foreknowledge of election to omniscience."[70] Miskotte had made this point repeatedly and emphatically. It is an important building block of his epistemology, which has taken cognizance of Nietzsche, Buber, and Barth.

Torah

The first key word in his *Bijbels ABC* is tôrāh (Torah) which Miskotte defines as "doctrine" [leer] or "holy teaching"—"holy" in the sense of particular, devoted, divine—which includes instruction. Unfortunately, Torah is often translated "law."[71] Paul's recurrent polemic against the νομος further contributes to misunderstanding.[72]

In his exposition Miskotte bases his comments on what he considers a true understanding of the Tanak. He does not enter into polemics with those who follow Luther's interpretation of Paul. Neither does he specifically endorse the teaching of Calvin, though his own views are closer to Calvin than to Luther.

Miskotte neither wants to understand the Torah in pagan nor in Jewish terms. Paganism as the natural religion of the human heart later produced, in addition to myth and cult, "teaching"—but always as explanation of the world, as examination of the riddle of the world. Judaism resorts to moral admonition, as an expansion and application of the system of justice of a holy people.[73]

Thus, Torah is to be broadly conceived. The term itself is flexible, referring to all of the books of the Pentateuch, or to all of the Tanak (John 10:34). At first sight, the Torah looks quite chaotic and its materials are presented in a heterogeneous fashion: not only historical and prehistorical narratives, sagas, hymns, but also laws, genealogies, etc.,[74] which cross the boundaries the world has set; even "those who are blind by nature will not err."[75]

Miskotte claims that formally and functionally Torah and Gospel are analogous; from the written record we proceed to the narrative, thence to the message (kerygma). In both the sequence is: from reading to seeing and hearing.[76] In a profound sense, however, the movement is from "event" (something that has happened) to "event" (something that is meant to happen).[77] Thus, the Word has both a past and a future.

In the Torah we also find commandments which must be seen as related to his presence, a gift of his covenant. He is the Liberator, who calls his people to walk with him. "All this is your story, your history with Me; no, rather, My story, My history with you!"[78]

A dichotomy between Law [Torah] and Gospel is inconceivable to Miskotte. "In the Torah we see the "law" passing over into "gospel" and the "gospel" passing over into "law;" so the "promise unfolds into commandments and so the commandments are bound up into the promise."[79]

To learn [lernen] is "a salutary duty" for we cannot raise ourselves (as Miskotte claimed in chapter 1). Diligent learning is intended to lead to experience; via our listening, we are led.[80]

In chapter 1 reference was made to the fact that Miskotte attended catechism for seven years. During his Haarlem pastorate (1930–1938) he wrote a spirited article entitled "The Significance of Catechism" in which he echoes many sentiments that remain relevant today.[81]

Learning, says Miskotte, is divine teaching, in which we find:

a) what is righteous (Hebrew: ṣedeq),
b) judgment, and
c) the direction, pointed out to us.

While he does not cite John's gospel, he might have referred to John 9:39 where Jesus is saying: "For judgment I came into this world. . . ." Miskotte writes: "Truth is not intended to be looked at, it causes a separation, it forces decisions, a choice, one way or another. Truth is the open action of God, which meets our spirit . . . which presents itself as presence, which comes to judge . . . our closed, lonely, wild spirit, to reject it, and cure it."[82] He is particularly critical of the Protestant churches and the loathing of church people to accept authority because, as he says, anarchy resides in the heart of the good citizen.[83] Continuing his exposition, he affirms the unambiguous need for authority (of the Word); thus, "teaching is to be directed under the salutary power of him who alone knows the right(eous: ssedeq) and who alone needs to judge and alone is able to give direction to our lives."[84] In the Dutch original (*Bijbels ABC*, 23), he plays with the verbal root *richten* which is recognized in English "right" and "righteous" and in German "recht" and "richtig" but all are contained in the Hebrew root ṣdq: ṣedeq is "right, righteous, straight" and the ṣaddîq is the man who reflects the qualities described by ṣedeq.

As mentioned above, all of the Bible is Torah, both the Old and the New Testament, "in that rich spirit-directed, life-moving sense. . . . Everywhere something is to be learned, living may be learned, learning what is life and what creates life, and how we must live." The godfearer is repeatedly exhorted to meditate on the Torah, day and night (Ps. 1:2; 24:4,5; 86:11).[85]

How does that relate to the Barth/Miskotte view of revelation? Out of Scripture proclamation, address, creative address raises itself—from God to his people: the happening of the eternal Word, in other words: revelation. Miskotte denounces what he labels a distorted interpretation of revelation as the communication of supernatural knowledge or knowledge about the supernatural.[86]

Revelation is about the Name. It is profoundly related to Torah, but not in the sense of a philosophy or a body of teaching. But it would be caricaturing Miskotte's view to suppose that revelation is the magic, single moment of divine-human confrontation, period (as in a sudden, one-time conversion). He never tires of stressing the need for instruction. Thus, in the church, besides the ministry of Word and sacrament there is catechesis. "It is truly nonsense to think that catechesis stops with 'confirmation.'"[87]

In his pastoral practice, Miskotte invested a great deal of time and effort in what we would call Bible studies. As we have seen, in his Haarlem parish some faithful members transcribed his teachings on the books of Job and Ruth (see chapter 1, "The Pastorate.").

The church as Servant of God is at once subject and object of this teaching, it is busy with *lehren* and with *lernen*. This takes place mutually. The teaching office is not a monolithic task. The church remains disciple (though she is charged with the apostolate) for she is not to be equated with the Kingdom of God. "The teaching remains, not only as a depositum, but also as a guide. Thus, there is every reason for us, inspired by the synagogue feast of the Joy of the Torah (*Simchat Torah*), to experience and to celebrate the joy of instruction."[88]

> Instruction (Torah) is not self-contained, resting in itself, but it contains the impetus to all good works, which are to the glory of God, according to his commandment, done out of true faith and not out of our own pleasure. Instruction is not one-sided, it is a form in the service of truth as we can understand it where words are used to indicate the riches of God's glory; it does not establish a party, it gathers a people: the new humanity. Instruction is not monotonous, for the unity by which it is recognized and distinguished from other teachings does not depend on its repetition, but in the joining together to achieve a polyphonic sound.

Continuing his musical metaphor, he says that instruction is like a symphony: many scores, one work, or like an orchestra: many instruments, one piece of music:[89] "Wherein lies the power of Scripture: to *lead* the spirits? In this, that they initially pass by the problems which we bring up, to tackle the unspoken need of life which is estranged from God; that they thus somewhere speak, self-contained and one-sided . . . of the bare fact: God is!—this dizzying fact by which life is not only illumined differently, but changes its direction."[90]

As if this were the "practical application" part of a sermon, Miskotte ends this important chapter with a special appeal to his contemporaries. Though this was penned a half a century ago, it would be difficult to deny relevance for our time. Modern man, he claims, as a member of the "lonely crowd," drifts along in his neutrality.[91] He cites Gerardus van der Leeuw for anecdotal evidence: "The slow loosening of every bond, religious, moral and national, has been and remains a great evil. It delivered our people defenselessly to genuine nihilism. . . . Grandfather was an elder, father attended church now and then, the son did not bother with anything, . . . the grandson became a member of the Dutch Nazi Party [N.S.B.], the party of the embittered and disillusioned."[92]

Miskotte suspects, and he has written about this more fully in *When the Gods are Silent* (fifteen years later), that so-called "neutralism" was for many the prelude to some sort of nihilism. Contrasting to what he said about the Word, he claims: "In that there is surely no onesidedness, but rather a chaotic multi-sidedness [al-zijdigheid: all-sidedness], no monotony but a cacophony of sounds."[93] What a commentary on our time with its ungovernable cities, diffuse parliaments, and smorgasboard theologies!

Miskotte ends with a quote from Buber in which he speaks of the word "in every time, which keeps its power, to grasp those who listen to it. Time is passive, the Word active. . . . It wants to speak, at any time. . . ."[94]

The Way

This keyword receives hardly any attention in the Old Testament theologies. Miskotte studiously avoids Hebrew words in his *Bijbels ABC*[95] but it seems quite clear that he is not dealing with hălākāh,[96] but with derek, (דֶּרֶךְ),[97] Greek οδος, which he puts in the context of the relationship between the "acts" and "words" of God. They are inseparable; the word is first, the act illustrates the word; or else, the act may precede; in that case, the word illuminates the act. The acts of God are part of the proclamation of his attributes (promise, prophecy, proclamation, exhortation). But there is no perfect balance between them: the prevenient word tips the scales. The promise is more decisive than the exhortation. The essential part is that God is believed for the word he speaks (John 13:19).[98]

Miskotte stresses "way" as a "primary word" [oerwoord]. This word needs to be understood in its Wortfeld. In one of his congregational newsletters (in Cortgene, in 1924), Miskotte wrote a series entitled "Van verborgen omgang" which is roughly translated as: "Concerning hidden relationship (or [reciprocal] communication)."[99]

The "way" is about the salvific secret of history: " . . . only by the knowledge of his ways do we come to the knowledge of the living God, as he goes through the world."[100]

"The way of all flesh," the human way, was not the original way. But at any time, mankind is called upon to drink from the chalice of time, to learn something about the way of God.

To Miskotte, "way" suggests motion. He goes so far as to call God a "God on the move [Trekgod], a leader of nomads." Once more he insists that we need to move from the particular to the universal: via God's way we learn to know his essential divinity, not the other way around. "God, YHWH, has a way, and creates room for himself, while traveling along to the eternal city, making his people fellow-travelers with him. . . ."[101] Thus, Immanuel means: *God is coming along with us.*

Again, Miskotte demonstrates his more-than-passing acquaintance with the scriptural text. In the Dutch church, Psalm 25, in its rhymed version, is wedded to a singable (and beloved) tune, and is therefore often used in worship. In this Psalm, *derek* functions as a significant keyword. Note that *derek* = (German) Weg.

> 25:4 *Your ways,* [deine **Wege**] YHWH, make me know your paths, teach me.
>
> 25:5 *Lead me* [Lass . . . deine **Wege** erkennen] in your truth and teach me, for you are the God of my "salvation."[102]
>
> 25:8 Good and upright is YHWH, (therefore) he teaches sinners *in the way* [in dem **Weg**]
>
> 25:9 *He leads* [lehrt seinen **Weg**] the humble in the right, and instructs the poor his *way.* [seinen **Weg**]

The verbal and noun forms where the root *drk* occurs in the Hebrew text have been printed in italics. It will be noted that our typical English translations make no consistent attempt to stay with a literal rendering of the Hebrew text. By way of comparison, Buber's German renderings have been added in brackets (with the key word דֶּרֶךְ in bold face: **Weg**), illustrating a clear advantage in his concordant translation in terms of its faithfulness to the Hebrew text.

This poem illustrates the dynamic character of *derek.* In vv. 4 and 5 the poet prays to "the God of his salvation" that he somehow put him on the (right) *derek;* he uses three verbal forms, which move roughly in the same Wortfeld: "know" (hiphil), "teach" (twice), and "lead" (hiphil verbal form of *drk*).

In vv. 8 and 9, the psalmist's prayer has been heard. He opens with a doxology: "good and upright is YHWH!" Two familiar verbs, used in the petition in vv. 4 and 5, recur: "lead" (hiphil verbal form of *drk,* 5a) and "teach" (4b, 5a). Interestingly, in v. 10 instead of *derek,* the poet has ›oraḥ, but it clearly functions as a synonym: "All the *paths* of YHWH are ḥesed wĕ›emet for the keepers of his bĕrît and his 'ēdôt." Are we permitted to draw the conclusion that those who walk in the *derek* (characterized as ḥesed wĕ'emet) follow the Torah of YHWH?

This brief excursus is given only to suggest that Miskotte tried, and seems to have succeeded, to keep his theology as *close to the words of Scripture* as he was able to.[103] Miskotte did not go into as much detail on Psalm 25 as given here, but he cites a number of other passages before he comments that God is *on the march:* a leader of nomads—an apt metaphor for the Christian life. God invites people to be fellow-travelers with him, not as an adventurer or a stay-at-home, but to be faithful in moving toward the goal, obedient to the word and watching the acts of the Lord.[104]

Conclusion

In chapter 1 of this work Miskotte was introduced, the man and his work. It may now be possible to offer some summarizing comments. The one thing that makes him stand apart from almost all of his confrères/theologians is that he was a literatus. Of course, professionally he was a pastor and a theologian, in his case to be understood as a hendiadys. Even that point is not without ambiguity, however, for there is a sense in which he resisted the pastorate and that he was, as it were, "forced" into it by practical considerations[1] but he has also acknowledged that he was called to that office while he was still a child.[2] Thus, he entered on his first pastorate with a certain amount of anxiety and even resistance. In that, too, he rings true; the call narratives of Moses (Exodus 3) and Jeremiah (Jeremiah 1) may serve as prototypes of his own call experience.

In the pastorate, he received a strong, practical impetus toward theology; in fact, it was his pastoral experience where the indissoluble nexus between Bible and theology was forged for him. In the best of the Reformed tradition (à la Calvin), theology was understood to be, as a matter of course, biblical. The remarkable thing is that, in spite of a less than inspiring theological education, he persisted in his biblical studies without any pretense of being a professional biblical scholar, but rather as something that, it went without saying, was part and parcel of the pastoral ministry. At the same time, his theological evolution, which was already notable during his student days,[3] progressed apace, for he remained an ardent reader. Quite early in his career, he wrote a work which may be considered a respectable contribution on biblical exegesis.[4] He accepted the then current historical criticism but also insisted that such criticism itself should be viewed critically.[5] Like Barth who spoke of Scripture's "own world," so Miskotte spoke about the Bible which "opens up like a world."[6] Translated into the language of our time, that means the practice of "close reading" and the study of language and idiom as well as the given structure of pericopes and biblical books, together with their respective contexts.

His repeated insistence that we need to move from the particular to the universal, from the specific revelatory event before making affirmations which are based on these events, has been referred to a number of times. It fits in with his aversion to ontology and his having taken to heart the caveats of Feuerbach and Nietzsche. His stance also finds solid support in the modus operandi of Scripture itself, where we are first introduced to specific revelatory events, before conclusions are drawn about the nature of the God who reveals himself. Accordingly, the affirmation "YHWH is God" is irreversible; elsewhere he says that the adjective (modifier) must not overgrow the substantive. Biblical theology moves from liberation (or redemption) to creation: the same God, who set his people free, is also the God who created all things.

Miskotte's exegetical endeavors avoided the trap in which biblical scholars sometimes fall, namely of becoming technicians with little or no reference to theology. Viewing Scripture through theological lenses, he was able to strike a balance between the practical needs of the pastorate and his development as a theologian.[7] Already while in his first pastorate (in Cortgene), while in his twenties, people from all over the country wanted copies of his parish paper. No faithful pastors who understand apostolic ministry will be very surprised at the tone of his farewell letter which he wrote to his parishioners in Cortgene.[8]

As indicated in this work, his relationship to Karl Barth remains something of a problem for scholars. Excellent primary resources are now available to those who wish to study the matter; they are Miskotte's diaries (*Dagboeken*), two volumes of which have been published in Verzameld Werk, with a third volume promised for publication in 1996,[9] Volume 2 of his Verzameld Werk (which contains much information on his relationship with Barth) and, last but not least, the Barth-Miskotte *Briefwechsel*.[10] Overall, he is rightly seen as a loyal supporter and interpreter of Barth whom he considered his master and teacher. Barth was to him the Hercules of evangelical theology, who virtually singlehandedly demolished the liberalism epitomized by theologians of the stripe of Adolf Harnack.[11] Miskotte had independently come to the conclusion that a new beginning was needed. When some of the notes struck in Barth's *Römerbrief* fell on Miskotte's ears, there was initial shock. When he kept reading, he become converted to Barth's view and came to think of Barth as "the theologian of the century," the one who succeeded in awakening Western Christendom from its liberal slumbers.

But Miskotte also went his own way in carving a niche for himself, chiefly in his preoccupation with Judaism and his concern with nihilism. Apparently, his interest in Judaism had deep roots, going back to his mother who professed her love for the Jews while raising her children.[12] Additionally, the Reformed milieu in the Netherlands in which he lived was more supportive of a mentality that would make ample room for the Old Testament.[13] During World War II, the Miskottes hid Jews from the long arms of the Nazi military. That Miskotte himself was spared from the Nazis' brutal arm in view of his (spiritual) brand of resistance, is amazing in itself.

His study of Judaism (as in his dissertation, *Wezen der Joodse Religie*) has appropriately been characterized as phenomenological.[14] Muis speaks of phenomenology as a kind of intellectual "halfway house" between empiricism and the truth question.[15] It was a good place to be for a scholar, at least temporarily. But Miskotte moved well beyond that; actually, he did so already on the first page of his book, where he bluntly claims that Judaism must not be regarded as a Vorstufe to Christianity but that it deserves to be accepted as an independent system of faith. That assertion struck the keynote not only for his study of Judaism, but for his preoccupation with the Old Testament as well. After his study of Jewish theologians in his dissertation, as the Nazi threat began to loom large on the eastern horizon, he penned *Edda en Thora* (1939),[16] which was, in a sense, resistance literature(!)[17] even before the Nazis crossed the Dutch border (within only a year!). Miskotte turned out to be something of a prophet; as an astute student of culture, he had a remarkable sense of the temper of the times, sensing quite accurately the nature of the Nazi threat to Western Europe generally and to the Jewish population particularly.

Another overriding concern of his was the loss of biblical faith which he witnessed during his lifetime,[18] in large part through his reading. Thus, his commitment to Christian faith was not only a matter of the heart, but just as much (one is tempted to say in Miskotte's case, even more so!) a matter of the mind. In this context, communicating the faith (particularly to intellectuals, to those who reflected on it) shows up as his agenda not only in his magnum opus, but also as a natural part of the office of the pastorate.[19] However, he was not interested in gimmicks. He felt that "building the church" by way of preaching and teaching (including the young by catechizing, which he took very seriously) was also the method of leading people to faith. His church, realizing Miskotte's solid commitment to what we might like to call "evangelism," appointed him to a post in Amsterdam. When he was subsequently made a professor by his church, it seems that all his life had been preparation for his greatest work, *When the Gods are Silent.* This work combined all his chief interests: modern literature, biblical theology, Judaism, and nihilism. Though he begins with a concise exposition of certain types of nihilism, interlaced with comments which offer a glimpse of what was to come, he soon begins to "unpack" his witness, bolstered by "interpretation"; this becomes the bulk of the book and its essential thrust. To say that *When the Gods are Silent* is a book about the preaching of the Old Testament is an oversimplification; it also offers a degree of cultural as well as theological and biblical sophistication for the benefit of those who are charged with the apostolate. Thus, when Miskotte faces nihilism, Nietzsche is in the background, yet he virtually avoids polemics, except to comment that many nihilist fellow-travelers (hedonists and utilitarians) land in the swamp of pessimism.[20] For the rest, he takes seriously, and simply inventories, the shambles left by Nietzsche: a dead God (irrevocably so), morality with nothing behind it, with the disappearance of the classical concept of truth. The death of God leads to nihilism, which in turn leads to "the self-surmounting of nihilism in eternal recurrence."[21] That is, of course, no longer biblical religion but a fundamental motif of nonbiblical religion where man may be the victim of, as Eliade put it, the "terror of history."[22]

A man of the stature of Miskotte radiated his influence in many directions. His multi-faceted interest provided him with a hearing among many who had little or no use for church and Christianity. Amsterdam was, and remains(!), his city. He spent his happiest years there. He preached the sermon immediately after the Netherlands were liberated in May, 1945. He led a prayer service for the convening of General Synod after a three-century hiatus. From Amsterdam he was called to be a University professor.

As has been pointed out, he has roots in all of the Reformed theological faculties: he studied theology in Utrecht, took his doctorate in Groningen, and taught at Leiden. Though he never taught in

Amsterdam, perhaps his greatest influence was in that city. Appropriately, the "Amsterdam School" (of biblical exegesis)[23] hails him as one of the significant founding figures.[24] G. H. ter Schegget claimed that Miskotte was the great inspiration of the Amsterdam School, "not the founding father, but the silent strength behind it."[25] While the present standard-bearer of the Amsterdam school is Karel Deurloo, Professor of Old Testament, University of Amsterdam,[26] the late Frans Breukelman is remembered as an inspiring founder of the developing Amsterdam School.

In a paperback containing an article by Miskotte and a number of additional contributions (presented at a Miskotte symposium), Breukelman told how as a young liberal pastor he served as an assistant to a minister of more evangelical leanings. When he had to catechize, he used Kittel's *Geschichte Israels:*

> So I simply expounded what the historian thought he could say about it (the Bible). What the historian knows is true: not what is found *in* the text, but what one may suspect *behind* the text. . . . At that time *Bijbels ABC* was an enormous liberation for me. . . . Miskotte showed us how the text speaks directly to a person. The truth manifests itself immediately in the text. Just read! Just listen! It is everywhere. Thanks to *Bijbels ABC* I experienced that it could be done this way. We did not need to crawl laboriously behind the text to reconstruct the truth. . . . Between all those suspicions and probabilities Miskotte comes simply to demonstrate that one can say how it is directly from the text itself.[27]

Clearly, Breukelman, who was known, almost to the time of his death in 1993 as a very enthusiastic teacher of Old Testament, acknowledges his dependence on Miskotte. Basically, it is this (in his words): "biblical theology originates with the Tanakh; [but] it is also the theology of the apostles."[28] Regardless of whether one prefers Barth or Miskotte, writes Breukelman, "with Barth a decision was made, a decision which may well be more significant than the decision of the 16th century. It is the same decision which was made in Barmen about the simplicity, salvation [heil], the one NAME, the one covenant, the matter around which everything revolves, the one future. . . . This decision signifies a total change of structure."[29] Breukelman then speaks of the Trinity, Christology, the divine attributes (from the general to the particular). But, as also seen by Karl Barth, that is not how Scripture operates. For Miskotte, the particular leads to the universal. "In the midst [there is] vere deus, who inclines to our depth, the faithful God who keeps faith (haššômēr 'emet), who is true God in that he wants to risk [inzetten] his divinity for humanity."[30]

And finally, one more testimony about Miskotte's contribution to biblical exegesis by Breukelman: "He has repeatedly demonstrated, suggested, offered, allowed [us] to experience, that it is possible to get one's bearing in the confusion of contemporary life and the present world from the text itself; the delightful experience, that expectations are nurtured, word and answer spring directly from the texts in today's world."[31]

Breukelman communicated almost exclusively orally. When he began to write, he shared his work by way of stenciled copies—lots of them.[32] Toward the end of his life, he embarked on a project of writing a biblical theology. So far, only three volumes have been printed[33] but a committee has plans to publish the remainder of Breukelman's works. Now that some exegetical work from scholars of the University of Amsterdam, who work in the spirit of Miskotte, is in print in the United States,[34] it is hoped that the Miskotte influence will eventually be disseminated in English-speaking countries as it is being promoted in the Netherlands.

Miskotte offers a catharsis in theology. Anyone who has read him with growing agreement, may also begin to view with growing dismay the muddle in which the American church finds itself. Sloppy theology spawns shoddy teaching, superficial preaching, and careless parishioners. Many have cheerfully traded their Christianity for some form of ideology or for another faith. No wonder that those who feel called to Christian ministry are confused. Those who are in earnest about that ministry and who are often just as confused as the rest, often meander by the smorgasboard that offers an incredible variety of theological options; the tasting is going on endlessly, often without arriving at any satisfactory conclusions that seem worth holding on to.

Miskotte was never in America, though he was once invited to Harvard. Even if he were here he would not be so naïve as to claim to have all the answers. But he is surely a potent reminder to those who have ears to hear that the effectiveness of the church and her apostolate stands and falls by the quality of a theology which is capable of inspiring authentic, biblical faith among Christian people of various traditions, . . . those who lead and those who follow.

Appendix A: *Edda en Thora*, Chapter 1

K. H. Miskotte

Een vergelijking van germaansche en israëlitische religie (Kampen: J. H. Kok, 1983, third printing)

Private Translation by Martin Kessler

Since the ground of faith [Glaubensgrund] has been carried off, Western institutions float in the air.

—Niekisch

The ones I called, the spirits
I cannot get loose from

—Goethe, *Zauberlehrling*

I) Science, whatever else it may be about, is in any case the art of naming. Name signifies distinction, connection, ordering: the annexation of the foreign, the relating of the unknown to the somewhat known, the absorption in a teleological relationship of older, valid naming. For knowledge (which begins with experience) is causality introduced in visible representational images or visible representational images brought into a causal relationship. The former pertains chiefly to the natural sciences, the latter to the humanities.

It speaks for itself that one investigator believes that there are too many names, and another that there are too few; the one, inclined to deduction, misses unity, the other, inclined to induction, already sees in the initial unity of order arbitrariness and violence. Leaving aside whether the "knowing" that is consolidated in the names is not always a different kind of knowing, to name a speaking, a naming, a relationship-creation, and connection-discovering will ever be the goal of observation and thought. But again and again, the question [14] relating to the too strict or too open relationship becomes acute, and thus the sense of naming.

What will ultimately dominate depends in part on the nature of the area of the science; in natural science, the relationship of data will dominate to the extent that their reduction to a few names is likely to dominate. With the humanities we rather encounter irreducable data, and one may likely join a certain pluralism, depending on the stage of development in which a special science finds itself. In the case of a young science, at least in the area of humanities or cultural science, a point of view of unity will be difficult to find, particularly if it understands its mission not so much to explain as to understand.

II) There are, however, also factors of an extra- and pre-scientific nature which relate to the decision whether we are called and are able to progress to greater unity in a determined limit of scientific reflection, or whether, precisely the reverse, it will be necessary to break through the order that was found. We never find ourselves with our science in a supra-historic, supra-temporal area. Apart from the relation of our striving for knowledge in practice, the technique of the engineer, the physician, the judge, etc., thought itself is not "free" in the sense, that it could place itself outside changing, personal, and societal human existence. An element of choice and of decision will obtain in the ordering of data.

To use the mysterious word, it is at least the "spirit of the age" [tijdgeest] which intervenes here with superior power, [15] and then, as is to be expected, more in the humanities than in the natural sciences, though the latter will also appear as not completely independent. One does not need to be committed to a theory concerning the closeness of cultural circles, one does not need to deny the idea of humanity at all, to grant that each more or less isolated science is receptive to certain prejudices, born or grown or strengthened by the suggestion of the spirit of the age. This is to be expected. In our time this dependence can be seen by the crowd; its ruined reputation is shamefully visible.

Yet, there is another side to this shameful dependence, namely, a possible realistic mentality with an eye on the future.

The history of culture, anthropology, and the history of religions are particularly affected by fluctuations in general intellectual life, and in an honorable way hang together with the real existence of people in a specific time frame, with its kairos, turns, and chances. We believe that we are presently thrown into a crisis in which, in spite of the catastrophic breakdown of much that is systematic, a "new" ordering of "names" is forcing itself on us, which harmonizes with the most recent knowledge, what the most ancient wisdom has felt, and what poets have prophesied.

III) Those who have become accustomed to think in the categories of experimental psychology or structural psychology suddenly discover that there are (measured by the latest norm) [16] only three types of people, namely *pagans, Jews, and Christians,* thus indicating realities which are more powerful and broader than those of the psychology of people, of ethnology, or psychoanalytical depth-soundings.

We see that when we neither lose ourselves in search of variants and symbioses, nor from a certain, quasi-objective ratio, exclude all of the religious life as belonging to a previous historical period—we see "images," [gestalten] "types," which to a degree are irreducable in themselves, which in no case can be derived from each other, therefore: ultimate religio-anthropological data. At the same time we discover how much the power of these realities relativizes the other data of people, race, history, culture, world view. Three worlds, three names!

This vision is shared by those who self-consciously call themselves pagans, not in a negative sense, but as confessing members of the anonymous pagan fellowship who then need to declare what in any case has become impossible for them. They say: "God can no longer be valid, the God who originated in the desert." That is less than heresy and more than rebellion, for heresy is a more or less reflected one-sidedness within the context of the church, and rebellion is incidental resistance to the acts of a government or hegemony, which one does not totally deny in principle. With differences in race we have so little to do, so that all races without distinction appear inclined to this rejection of God. This is new.

This is rather a renewed encounter with another God, [17] our own God, his power in us and over us; it is the rediscovery of ourselves under the rubble of beings which were covered by the centuries. Here a new "name" lives.

Many have supposed that when the Imperium Romanum declined, an Oriental madness came over the nations which led to the justification and glorification of anarchist instincts. The close relationship of religion with country [vaderland] broke because of this Oriental import; more clearly: by Christendom, more honestly: by this unknown, strange, disturbing God, who is no respecter of persons.

Fustel de Coulanges (in *La Cité antique*) described the event like this: "the soul had no country anymore and heaven had no weapons anymore." It was more clearly seen what had been lost by the victory of Israel's God over the West. All others who did *not* complain about what was lost, were grouped together.

[18] Nietzsche grouped together Christ, Luther, Savonarola, Rousseau, and Robespierre as "epileptics of understanding." All of them are unbound, sharing in orgies, chiliasts, and atheists in the ancient sense, without god. For this foreign God is more than "god," according to the attributes which are ascribed to him, but less in that the natural heart does not know what to do with him: what are we to do with the Stranger?

The Roman Church, according to the school of Charles Maurras and also according to the George-Kreis, must be appreciated as the keeper of a certain balance between Jewish "monotheism" and the ancient thought world. Outside of this church, however, monotheism appears to be a threat to every political order. When the tired European spirit, after the terror of the Enlightenment of another century, looked through the windows of Romanticism to new lands and new sources of life, then according to these spokesmen a new self-betrayal took place, though precisely at that point it became obvious that a division dominated the European spirit, a division [19] which was originally caused by the "foreign God," the Oriental import. Thus one can understand that the resistance to the God of Israel and the longing for form and bond, image and authority became more and more identical in the German prewar youth movement.

When disaster clenched its fists, Spengler, the prophet of doom, dragged along a disappointed people in his apocalypses, and the Baltic Count Keyserling, tired of all of the West, opened new vista toward Indian and Chinese spiritual values. The "Russian soul" undoubtedly exercised the greatest influence by means of Dostoyevsky; Tagore and Gandhi were briefly honored; if in all of this there was the ferment of decline, when it did not bring satisfaction, the spirit sank back under its own weight in the maternal grounds of its own paganism.

Add to that, that since then the world, which had technically become a unity, fell apart spiritually in a multitude of autarchic strivings; clearly, no general religiosity can satisfy this generation. The call for a genuine god of one's own resounds everywhere. The profound "names" bring separation.

Theoretically one would not easily decide for this possibility: that the most cerebral time thinks it can overcome relativism in such a naïve way! Nevertheless, we stand before undeniable facts. . . .

> Youth calls for the gods. Rise up
> Fill the days as if eternal. Guiding
> In stormy clouds, he gives to the one of the bright sky
> The scepter, and displaces the longest winter.
> [20] Who was hanging on the tree of salvation, threw down
> The palest of the pale souls; to the dismembered
> As with passionate frenzy, Apollo secretly leans
> on Baldur: "For a while night continues,
> But this time light comes not from the East."
> The battle was already decided in the stars. Victor
> remains he who hides the protective image in his heart
>
> (Stefan George, *Das Neue Reich,* 34)

Line five alludes to Odin, who hung on the world tree in German mythology, while the words: "Apollo leans secretly on Baldur" speak for themselves, as a new religious consciousness is expressed by the sentence: "but this time, light does not come *from the East.*"

IV) The 19th century did *not* believe in the simplex vere sigillum—and rightly so according to its mentality. It was gloomy and proud, both in the lower layers of its social striving as well as among the lonely, who wished to form a counterweight and antidote to the former, which inevitably brought with it the leveling of life and values.

It has discovered—in responsible scientific work, shrugging and delighted—something in the "given" of what the Latin spirit of Maurras tends to call "obscene infinity," originating in the "Hebrew desert and the German forest."

The "new man" sees, correctly from his standpoint, the fatal synthesis between Bible, mysticism, and humanism, grown into a monstrous force precisely in the 19th century. At a much later time, it was destined to treat the [21] incomparable, tragic greatness of that century with respect. For the time being, Wagner and Mahler, van Gogh and Cézanne, Tolstoy and Dostoyevsky, Eleonora Duse and Josef Kainz are the last of an era, a sunset, a final chord, followed by the dusk of epigones and the night of new (or old) chthonic powers. The torment of the infinite, the beauty of contrasts, the storm of spiritual ecstasies, the lofty flight of individuality, the tenderness of "impossible" longings, the clear resignation, the solemn silences of skepticism, the doom of relativism—they are all gone!

Our century is different; it flees from relativism back to an enclosed certainty, from humanity to the nation, from science to confession, from knowledge to choice, from the truth question to the discovery of reality, from futurism to surrealism and hyperrealism, from faithful questioning to a grim, supposed knowing.

The *shift of values* is great and can hardly be measured. Words like "simplicity," "virtue," "manliness," "earnestness," etc., come to signify the opposite meaning of what they meant in the language of the heroes of the 19th century, even if there have naturally also been precursors of the present, since the continuity of the spiritual life of humanity is certainly never completely broken.

Meanwhile, precisely this century, which has been so despised, has forged the intellectual tools for us with which we can understand and evaluate to some degree this movement and reversal. Even the despisers need to handle them, if only provisionally. That is precisely the enormity [22] and the oppressiveness of the situation, that an Urleben persists by means of spiritual-technical refinement. Deliberate separation is all the more necessary, with a clarification and a clarifying of the "names" from the inside out, so that they may at least be fixed.

A final offshoot of "morphology," of what Nietzsche not unpleasantly calls a "chemistry of human impressions," gradually becomes actual science.

If we give up the choice, the rightfulness and its motives, if we take the shift itself as a phenomenon, then such an attempt is praiseworthy because it is indispensable in order to consciously know our place in the struggle of this time.

Then it appears, in our opinion, that the heresy that appears so rough and gestures so wildly, or the rebellion or self-discovery, is, formally speaking, not so far beside the truth. . . . If on the one hand, things as they appear are still more complicated than we formerly thought, on the other hand basic structures come to the fore out of the pattern of data, which nearly agree with what the noisy vanguard of a new generation needs in prejudices. We arrive at a *simplifying of morphology*. We can agree in the determining of front lines, we hope for a separation of spirits.

The manner in which this simplification is reached, for example by a space and race [Raum-Rasse] theory as with Wilhelm Hauer [23] (*Deutsche Gottschau*, 1934)—may be subject to objections; yet we can learn something, insofar as such a simplification of morphology shows us something of the structure of Germanic thought. Thus we notice again and again that the handling of the teaching of form [gestaltenleer] itself shows something of the form to which the thinker belongs. The compulsion or inspiration, under which he stands, appears to well up from much deeper strata than logical insight, aesthetic appreciation or moral conviction. Nietzsche, who boasted of his "atheism," is indeed the seer of (new or old) world-dominating images of god [godsgestalten]. The simplification of morphology, taken by itself, offers a final, common platform for a debate [Auseinander-setzung]. As Christians we understand perfectly the words of a young fascist (1926): "We must feel firm ground under our feet, to us truths must be as honed swords made of the hardest steel. The so-called freedom of spirit has disappointed us badly, because it did not give us security instead of ancient truth, for it has only been able to bring forth 'principles.'" Between the confession of the God, whom Israel and the church have proclaimed, and rediscovered ancient truth, all religiosity, idealism, and morality are squeezed out. [24] What already characterized the first years of the 20th century is the secret farewell of German idealism, because the meaning of life was not found to be obvious in any way. Natorp and Simmel, who may be regarded as the greatest representatives of that period as far as philosophy is concerned, have the greatest difficulty coming up with any kind of purposiveness for life.

This time calls for the gods. He does not build systems anymore; neither does he create any new gods; this is his profundity, that he calls the old gods. Perhaps it also seals his despair; but despair is a reality which belongs to none of the categories of this morphology, and about which it is not becoming to speak directly in such a study as this.

"The ancient gods will indeed return, but with a new face. Only their power over humanity and their laughter about the sins of world history will be the same. *They will return,* that is certain. The hour of their return will be the final hour of the Christian era." We believe that we do well to take this insight and vision seriously. We believe that the simplification [25] of morphology did not only become a formal possibility, but also that according to its content it had a certain general validity. It is possible to define what paganism, Judaism, and Christianity are, in such a way that pagans, Jews, and Christians can basically agree on the definition. An opposing axiology may be joined with a commonly defined and recognized morphology.

V) We surely need to reflect that teachings which are presented very fanatically do not always signify what is essential; in a broader syntax of ideas, they may be a rule or an exception, they may be a means toward a goal, which is not necessarily related to it. Thus we see the racial doctrine of . . . [Nazi] Germany, spiritually considered, in large part as an excuse of much deeper intentions. An unsuspected witness wrote in 1931: "All of William's people [wilhelminischen Menschen] begin consciously or unconsciously with racial doctrine as their starting point. . . ." Two years after Heilscher wrote this, this "Western defection" was the emblem of a revolution which pretended to liberate the people for a new spiritual life, precisely in the decisive aversion to the "West." With or without racial theory [26] as an appropriate political weapon, the dynamic line of intended movements therefore remains the same.

What we see occur before our eyes is nothing but a *crusade* against the "foreign God" of Israel (which is also the God whom the church confesses). More or less all theories, constructions, programs, and pedagogical systems serve this crusade. Therefore the greatest oppositions are spent, to leave room for the largest, the "final one," therefore the "new man" overcomes all reverses, therefore he can possibly see the threat to his position soberly without giving up his plan or utilize his energy more carefully. There is certainly a bitter *opposition* in *fascist* thought which in large measure explains its fanaticism; the hero on the one hand and the mass on the other do not fit together, a government of aristoi and an acknowledgment (even if it be pedagogical) of all plebeian instincts exclude one another, and where the relationship is yet tested, the opposition *in* this thinking will prove stronger than the opposition in which it has set itself to its "enemy" which is Bolshevism; if a relationship between enemies should become public, which would be denied by words, but affirmed by instincts and by the necessity of self-revelation sooner or later would become manifest. But even so, things continue.

No time and no societal realism are less fitting to make room for the heroism of the noble than precisely the time which we experience presently. Often we think that we find an anachronism in proclaimed teaching, [27] that tries in vain to block the stream of the times. . . . Nevertheless the dynamic strength of intended movements and strivings rather grows than diminishes by these hindrances.

Thus also racial theory (as proclamation for the masses) and myth are structural opposites; one must either mythologize race itself or banalize myth; and one does both by turns or both at the same time. Only a few thinkers know how to withdraw from this dilemma (as, e.g., Julius Evola); they are then automatically excluded from spiritual and political leadership, while precisely those who do not see any problem here . . . are able to maintain themselves as leaders for the time being. I) It appears to be a praiseworthy and fruitful striving to many humanistically oriented writers to prove the untenability of racial theory and its consequences from all sorts of perspectives; their work is easy. It does not appear fruitful to us, not so much because we believe that this biological theory is only a *first pawn* that is moved at the beginning of the game, which truthfully, at least in its intention, will be continued in a very different style. A sacral battle, a religious war in *optima forma* has begun and will, unless signs mislead, lead to the destruction of German and European culture.

There was a time when we could feel fortunate because of the indescribable riches of the German spirit, even where it was unclear and by its great depth appeared forever [28] doomed to immaturity. Beside the brooding Faust, Eulenspiegel the wise jester and Parcifal the "clean fool" were to us an essential image of the German soul. Worse than racial theory is the withering of these forms, which is more difficult to explain as an early move, a pretended, provisional phenomenon. Goethe has been infected by Spinoza the Jew, Schiller is a "Western internationalist," Rembrandt is the "opponent of our racial soul." This should not be called intellectual madness, for it is partly true. It is only madness in the sense of religious ecstasy, of the "mania" of which Plato spoke, of the furor teutonicus as enthusiasm, as being filled-with-God, as being possessed-by-oneself. One needs to have loved the delightful German people as the heart and conscience of Europe, one must owe to this people the best of one's culture, one must have tuned one's heart to the tone of the classical Lutheran church hymn to appreciate to some degree what is ruined with the takeover of this furor, this religious possession, which lies many fathoms deeper than the grounds which are claimed for racial theory and racial politics.

Thus, we need to meet the true values, to be "too righteous" and rather eliminate all racial theory; we wish to see the call for the gods, regardless of how it is mixed with this quasi-science, as of its own kind and in its own right.

We wish to honor paganism. We want to learn to see it anew. We want to gauge and accept the great simplification [29] which it presses upon us. A new earnestness is needed, an insight that splits the syntheses because paganism finds itself again. We wish to open each others' eyes for nonsensical associations which the word "paganism" has acquired among us. Paganism is *not* atheism; to the contrary, it is a very solid, mature [welgedaan] faith; paganism is not liberalism or libertinism, but to the contrary, communal life that is always oriented to the bonding and the honoring of the state; paganism is not backward, but to the contrary, it is the perpetual ferment of human life; also, there are not *many* pagan religions, and insofar as they exist, they understand one another perfectly, and may even provide an example of mutual tolerance. In short: paganism is *the* religion of human nature, always and everywhere.

VII) Probably many young intellectuals have no idea of the world-shocking pretense raised by the Babel-Bibel question around 1910. This entire complex of questions almost completely absorbed the attention of Old Testament scholars; it dominated the curriculum, divided the spirits, removed every attempt to arrive at a deeper approach to Old Testament problems.

But how things have changed since then! Whether scholars were in favor or against the Babylonian interpretation of the Old Testament, their questions back then concerned themselves ultimately with genetic problems, with priority and dependence. To be sure, these were related inextricably with the valuation of Old Testament religion, with its originality and finiteness, and finally with the question [30] of "special revelation." As such this philological investigation received the measure of theological reflection but it never, or hardly ever, became so serious as to become existential. For "paganism" was a distant and pale concept that one had to try to approach by "empathy" [Einfühlung] at the study desk and in the teaching chair. It was a "past" which was necessary as a ledger line [hulplijn], as side-construction for the explication of the origin of Old Testament writings. Who would have thought that this paganism—not the so-called "paganism" of the secularized West—forms a permanent element in all human spiritual life, who suspected that this paganism, instead of furnishing us with some interesting parallels for our study, would confront us face to face as modern "truth," as *reality of the people's soul,* as state-constructing religion, as "demonic" theocracy? Have assessments ever been turned upside down in such a short time in spiritual history, has the work of science (apparently) ever been annulled in such a brief time span, and the most practical conclusions recalled?

Whereas it was seen as libel in 1900 when mythical elements were indicated in some view, presently it is considered the great crime of Christendom that it has annulled mythology! If at that time pantheism could be given the honorific title of a critical philosophy, also by those who adhered to a totally difference epistemology, that happened because pantheism at any rate had accomplished the liberation of religion from myth. Presently, all has been turned upside down [31], precisely insofar as so-called "pantheism" evaporates divine forms, to that extent it is viewed critically, indeed, sometimes "Christian" or even called a product of world Judaism, which is nothing but a laborious way of saying: we find it disagreeable, we do not recognize our God in that, it is opposed to the Reality we experience, to the Power, which we must honor.

Myth itself becomes a god on whom one "bases" oneself, in whom one rests, with whom one has fellowship. The "numinous," till recently accepted as the purest description of a typical-religious feeling of life [levensgevoel], is now branded as an *Angst*-psychosis of mixed races and placed opposite to the Olympic, but also to the Odin-like, the Thor-character, the Frigga-type.

If one asks whether this is "genuine," "pure," "naïve"—what might be our answer? We discover that *"naïveté" is a complicated matter.* It is possible to suspect in the resuscitation of myth the "second religiosity," which Spengler expects shortly before the ruin of the West, in Christian forms. On the other hand the question whether the great so-called naïve periods, which are viewed at the same time as high points of cultural life, have not already been ambivalent. That, too, we judge as a gain [32] of this time, that we view the distinction of conscious and unconscious, of naïve and reflective differently. Conscious spontaneity, intentional naïveté, refined primitivism, do not appear impossible to those who have again come under the spell of an old god. Yet we let this matter rest and remain credulous of the forms in which the "new man" gives and presents himself.

VIII) One may support paganism naïvely and consciously, one may also reject it both naïvely and consciously. Certainly in form and development this makes a great difference, but in essence the decision made matters little either way. Here we touch the "existential," which relativizes the named contradictions. Therefore, we deem impossible in these questions any attitude which rejects the renewal of Germanic religion, but partly on opportunistic grounds, as we also reject the delusion which was still possible a short time ago, that the Edda [33] might only have poetic value "for us." Led by a few, many have come to realize that the myth is "our" myth, that something lives in us (if one prefers, "in our blood"), which recognizes itself in it, and thereby gladly joins the impulse of an inner necessity which hardly leaves room for choice and reflection. We are rather surprised that no more of the young might discover this.

It appears to us rather obvious that a realization predominates with the best and the most conscious, that our language has become too lean to interpret some more religious truth, that *the accents of what has been suppressed* can only be revived in the word symbols of myth, so that we, Germans, instead of being elevated once and for all above myth by the coming of "Christendom" rather—unless we have personally been converted—have sunk beneath the myth in a profane and unreal sphere of vitalism and utilism, in which ultimate meaning is lacking. We do not wish to condemn those who suffer in this unreal life. Too much in our life agrees with them, too much the resistance rages in us against the vacuous, against a world which extinguishes every spiritual earnestness. "New people" hate that world.

They look for a way back to a condition of free and unbroken life, in which people—according to Hamm's words—knew not yet the writing, but the painting, not yet the declamation, but the song, not yet religion, but magic—thus, not a way to the idyllic but to immediate and elementary-powerful life. [34]

That in fact these rediscoveries—horribile dictu—are in the service of the masses which never was in such malam partem massa as at this moment, that there is a wonderful contradiction between combating Christendom as a mass-religion and the endless reproach of "personality cult" and what else of this kind might be mentioned, we rather ignore this in consideration of good manners, though we know that reciprocity in such treatment may not be expected.

The issue is not to be right or wrong; it is therefore not our goal to point to the logical, ethical, and practical impossibilities (and therefore: violent deeds) which are ventured with a straight face in the current German regime. We only wish to show what paganism is, apart from the possible or impossible consequences which related to it in a fixed government system. Indeed, we see the inner impossibilities, in the style: "Because—thus he concludes trenchantly, Nothing can be, what may not be" (Chr. Morgenstern), yet it is quite instructive in our opinion to see what "may not be" according to the new mythology, and abstract therefore from the question, whether "it cannot be." The "nonsensical" is also phenomenologically meaningful, the "impossible" is also to be understood as possible and necessary from certain presuppositions.

Such "abstracting" we hold to be a scientifically defensible method . . . as well as a way in which humanity may be practiced even with the fiercest enemy.

Appendix B: *Bijbels ABC*, Chapter 9

K. H. Miskotte

(Baarn: Ten Have, 1992, 7th printing)

Private Translation by Martin Kessler

[108] How are the acts and the word of God related? They cannot be separated; the word precedes and the act illustrates the word; or, the act comes first and the word illustrates the act. The acts of God are *enclosed* as it were by the proclamation of his attributes (in promise and in prophecy, in proclamation, and in admonition). If one asks whether there exists a complete balance according to the ABCs, the answer needs to be: no; there is a decisive *surplus weight* of the word which precedes beyond the word which follows. The promise is more decisive than the admonition; the promise does not even cease when what was predicted has come about. The advance proclamation extended itself also to console those who lived in expectation before the coming of the fact, before the breakthrough of the act.

"I tell you this now, before it takes place, so that when it does take place you may believe that I am he" (John 13:19). It is of the essence to believe God, this God, at his word. It is of the essence that we walk "in the footsteps of the faith of our father Abraham," (Rom. 4:12) even if the fulfillment has come, and in the expectation that we do not need to do without the "signs," which during his life supported faith. The idiom shows, and the language speaks for itself that we do not believe in the acts of the Lord, but in the Word, and in the acts as they are proclaimed to us through the Word.

-2-

Meanwhile this description of the relationship of God's word and his acts are valid for us, according to the manner in which we understand them, also and particularly in our personal, spiritual life. But the Bible has an *Urwort*, a basic term, which is not often noted but which expresses precisely something characteristic of the sacred teaching, and underscores again its anti-pagan nature—we mean the word "*way.*" The way of God or the ways of God [109] are often accented with great emphasis, because fact and meaning, word and act, promise and event, and promise again, because the unity of God's act-as-word and God's word-as-act comes fully to the fore in it. We might also put it this way: the salvific secret of *history,* history as salvific secret, is indicated by this phrase: "the way of God." Knowledge concerning God always includes: trust concerning his ways. Or rather, only through the knowledge of his ways do we arrive at the knowledge of the living God, as he goes through the world.

-3-

An inextinguishable suspicion lives in us, that no matter how briefly, for an "eternal" moment the good has reigned on earth, because evil can only be imagined as denial of the good. Then the way of man began, "the way of all flesh." Is this only surrounded by an unmovable Being, who permits everything to happen, or does God participate in our suffering, on the way of our existence, in the *time* in which we live? Paganism, particularly when it sublimates itself to a philosophical world view, must ignore this question and must finally even learn: in the beginning was chaos—lying entangled from the beginning in a disturbed equilibrium and a constant alternating of good and evil, life and death. Out of evil comes good, from death life, and also the reverse; there is no warning of the one before the other. We, who allow ourselves to be taught by the sacred teaching and who want to learn how to spell the biblical plan, say: no, that cannot be true, as surely as the *Lord* is God.

The real is before the unreal, the true before the wrong, justice before injustice, life before death, not only in the eternal sense, but also in the *chronological order.* We cannot retrieve this mathematical line, so narrow, so rarefied, as if it were not there, in reality. And *that* there exists something like truth and justice in eternal validity—we can only know it from and through and in the Name, the Revelation, the presence of God. And when we know it, our longing begins to burn for the timeless reign of peace. If we remain in our place and obediently drain *the cup of time,* it is because we hear God's word in time, see his act and his sign in time, but above all because we learn to understand something about the way of God. What we view as "history," [110] looks like a breaking of reefs, the blowing of free tradewinds without purpose, a writing of the most tremendous things in the sand, indeed, with traces of blood, all of which nevertheless are wiped out. And *after* a bit of reality comes a sea of lies, *after* a glimmer of justice a chaos of injustice, *after* all of life and culture and dream, death; what do we profit then by our principal insight: that the true comes logically *before* the wrong, when the wrong in this practically celebrates its existence, that it has the longest breath in the order of time according to the saying: "He laughs best who laughs last." And *with that we are so terribly alone! We* are the only ones who have history, unlike animals or angels. Only where there is a beginning and an end, something may happen that may be called history. The Word falls here or there, the acts of God have taken place incidentally, back then. And the spaces between them? That is where *we* are and suffer in our lives more than we lead [Dutch wordplay: lijden = to suffer, and leiden = to lead: homonyms]. There we are in the tohuwabohu (Gen. 1:2) of dark possibilities. Are the acts of God set unattached in that alone, here and there and somewhere? Does there fall only here and there a word of God on earth? Or is there a connecting of moments, a course and a goal, of which we might know for our comfort? Animals and angels have no history,

but God has a history.

And man, who may know of that, never needs to be lonely, not even when the godless laugh, and even if they all laughed together and even if they would truly laugh last, it cannot be the best form of triumph.

-4-

Thus, we learn to spell the word "way" in the sacred teaching.

[The renderings below generally follow Miskotte's translations.]

"O Lord, your way is manifest in the sanctuary" (Ps. 73:17)

"Make me alive by your ways" (Ps. 119:37)

"The Lord created me [wisdom] at the beginning of his way" (Prov. 8:22)

"This God—his way is perfect" (2 Sam. 22:31; Ps. 18:22)

"In the path of your judgments, O Lord, we wait for you" (Isa. 26:8)

". . . neither are your ways my ways, says the Lord, for as the heavens are higher than the earth, so are my ways higher than your ways" (Isa. 55:8b, 9a)

"In the wilderness prepare the way of the Lord, make straight in the desert a highway for our God" (Isa. 40:3)

[111] "His way is in the whirlwind and in the storm and the clouds are the dust of his feet. He rebukes the sea, . . . the mountains quake before him, . . . the earth is elevated before his face, with the world and all that dwell therein" (Nah. 1:3–5)

"O the depth of the riches and wisdom and knowledge of God! How unsearchable are his judgments, and how inscrutable his ways!" (Rom. 11:33)

"and he [who sat upon the throne] said to me: It is finished! I am the Alpha and the Omega, the beginning and the end." (Rev. 21:6)

"They [the kings of the earth] shall sing of the ways of the Lord" (Ps. 138:5).

The science of history of religions says—it may sound disrespectful yet it is profoundly true—that YHWH is *a God on the march* [trekgod], a Leader of nomads. If we firmly keep in mind that this is part of his Name and his Revelation on earth, if we remember well that belonging to his name are the adjectives that describe his attributes: justice and mercy, wisdom and patience, and if we keep an eye on the fact that this specific, this figure, this particular activity, this figure, do not in the least conflict with his Omnipotence, Omnipresence, and Omniscience—then this description of a God on the march also becomes an expression of the direction of the way of knowledge, namely, from the knowledge of God's *Way* to the knowledge of his essential deity, and not the other way around. There are degrees in the presence of God; with a dying person he is different than he is to a young man in his spring time. He is present differently in history than in nature, differently in the world than in the church, and differently in the word than in the sign, but also

he is present differently today than in former ages.

That is why the Ark went along with Israel's army, that is why the carrying rods could not be removed from this traveling divine throne, that is why there was from the beginning in Canaan, when the people came to be settled, tension, friction, and finally a life-and-death struggle between the God-Leader and Baal the god-of-the-land. Those who are not a nomad in one way or another, literally or spiritually, who are dulled by the sultry charm of the existing, from the cycle of nature and the wheel of birth, do not know the way.

God, YHWH, has a way, and creates room for himself and, traveling along to the eternal city, he makes his people fellow-travelers *with him,* on the march, not as adventurers, not homebound, but faithful to the goal, obedient to the word, watching the acts of God. For this Restless One, who restlessly [112] moves in spite of his own eternal peaceful essence, knows what he wants in the tumult of those who fight for their freedom.

Thus, we may and must answer the question: Is there then no relationship between the moments? Do animals and angels have no history distinct from man as the only being that has history: YHWH has a history. He makes history for us and with us. His hope is our hope, his divinity is co-humanness. That means: God himself is in the act of his Being, history. That too lies enclosed in the name "Immanuel," God is going with us.

-5-

The *terrifying reality* of history hangs on the oneness of God's word and God's act, of salvific word and salvific fact. Nature in her darkest areas is not so real, nature knows no heaven or hell. Heaven and hell, blossoming, wilting, confirming, destroying, peace and non-peace are destinations, not of natural existence but of historical life.

The *delightful* reality of history becomes manifest in the Kingdom of God, that grows in the fields of history, or comes to pour forth and spread out across the fields of history. An "eternal return" could never bring forth anything new; no chain of reincarnations can replace the seriousness of goal-oriented history. People with inextinguishable *memory* go in history; *nations* have, "make," and undergo history. The seal of concrete history is *politics,* the struggle for justice in the community, the long way, which for that reason alone is no madness, because God has a Way over the *earth,* because the Name, revelation, employs Cyrus and Caesar Augustus and Pontius Pilate in their service. And if the Counter-Messiah, the Antichrist is ultimately a political figure, a world-renowned individual, the Messiah, the Christ is one no less; indeed, the counter-candidate would not get so exercised if the Messiah were not striding very decisively to the world's throne along the *way* of God. Here also the word precedes; it is proclaimed to us, it is taught us: thus, history obtains this depth for faith, and this horrifying and delightful reality.

-6-

[113] Listen to the prayer of adoration of Habakkuk (3:3) according to Shigionoth, "the manner of the raging." [Based on Miskotte's rendering.]

"God came from Teman, and the Holy One from Mount Paran. Selah (= worship!) His glory covered the heavens, and the earth was full of his praise. . . . Before him went pestilence, and the fiery ember *in his tracks.* He stood and measured the earth, he watched and dissolved the nations—the eternal mountains burst already, already the hills of yore were bending, the passing of the ages are his passing. . . . You have cleft the rivers of the earth, the mountains saw you and suffered pain; the waterstream plunged down, the abyss raised its voice. . . . The sun raised its hands on high and the moon stands still in her house, at the light of your flying arrows, at the spreading of glory by the lightning of your spear. *With fury you stride across the earth, in anger you thresh the people,* you march out to set your people free, to give freedom to your anointed . . . you pierce with your own lances the leader of the troops; they storm, to blow us away; their jubilation is this, that they can eat the poor in secret. There you tread the sea with your horses, in the breakers of the great waters. That is what I perceived and my body shook, my lips trembled under my cry. . . ."

Or, let us hear a profound conversation, in Exod. 33:11–14; it contains "teaching" about the Way: "And the Lord spoke to Moses face to face as a man speaks with his friend . . . and Moses said to the Lord: See, you say to me: Lead this people, but you do not let me know whom you will send with me, yet you have said: I know you by name! And also: You have found grace in my eyes! Now then, I pray, if I have found grace in your eyes, let me know *your way,* that I may know you, that I may find grace in your eyes; and consider, that this people is your people. He then said: Would my Face have to *go along,* to pacify you? Then he said to him: If your Face will not go with us, do not make us march from here."

-7-

The character of *defenselessness* and *powerlessness* carries the noblest appearances in this world. [114] But God's Way "knows" the just, the poor, the orphan, the widow, justice, those who are cut off, the hope of the miserable, the turtle dove (Ps. 74:19), the apple of the eye (Ps. 17:8; Zech. 2:8). Word and Act tend to the End, tend also to protecting and keeping and liberating these powerless people and defenseless expectations. The bare fact, so to speak, of God's existence, and permanence (as this God whose attributes we know in the Name, through the sacred teaching) not only enlightens history, but changes it. There is not only a speaking, not only an acting, but a word-act and an act-word, that describes a *course* across the earth, does a work and completes it, a work that is proportional in weight, indeed, more than proportional to creation in the beginning. It is the creation of the End, of the Sabbath, through the course of the anointed One (Ps. 89:52). There are divine footsteps, which as they are placed, indicate and authenticate a unique Happening.

-8-

Once more: for here it is clearer than anywhere else in the sacred teaching, that this Way also can only be understood correctly from within the Center, from the place where YHWH established a memorial for his name (Exod. 20:24), where his track is found in history, where his special way has carved its own channel in human existence. These are junctions, which no one can ever completely forget, not so much because a holy past hovers around them, but because beyond them the "Way" ran farther to open a future for humanity. They are midpoints and media. They speak in the midst of time that God is "holy" (i.e., different from the world and the gods). Finally, we are invited to keep in mind the decisive center (2 Tim. 2:8) and to celebrate Jesus' life as the holiest past and the holiest future. "Do this in remembrance of me" (Luke 22:19; 1 Cor. 11:24) and "then you proclaim the death of the Lord with an eye on his future" (1 Cor. 11:26; Rev. 3:20). In him the fullness of the godhead dwells bodily, in him the Lord goes our way in the flesh and yet it is par excellence his Way. The

Name manifested in the humiliation, in the "lowest parts of the earth," in "the likeness of sinful flesh" is itself called the Way. Then the Way is parallel with Truth and with Life. "I am the Way, the Truth and the Life." There are already [115] footsteps on earth which are never eradicated. That is where God has taken our life and our death on himself, where he has become partaker of our lot even to the point of outer darkness. If we look back from Jesus Christ to the Old Testament, only then does this become truly *alive* for the first time as a witness of the God who makes his way across the earth, so that he may finish his work at the End and will be glorious in all of his saints and in the world.

-9-
Liberation

Someone will ask: What is then the real intention of God's own way in the world? He always presupposes evil and misery (which cannot and may not be explained). The Hebrew verbal stem from which the words: redemption, salvation, rescue have been derived, means: *to make room, to create room, to fix room,* namely for humans who are pressed, in distress, in anxiety, in anxiety of death. The best rendering is: liberate and liberation. Thus, Buber consistently translates "freedom" where the old translation has "salvation," [heil] thus: liberation. The general tendency of the notion of freedom may occasion a slackening of the notion: liberation. Therefore, in "liberation" we need to think also of the depth of distress, threat, death, the entire world of dark powers—signs of perishing, as gates of hell, "She'ol," the netherworld, the realm of shades, non-life. Here the biblical ABCs make no distinction between personal and communal need, between spiritual and physical distress; the ultimate concern is about humanity and the threat to its existence and about this God who works "liberations in the midst of the earth" (Ps. 74:12). " The voice of the earth goes up *de profundis* (=out of the depths, Ps. 130:1) because humanity is not destined to be cut off from life, of space, of possibilities of living before the "face" (the directed presence of YHWH, e.g., Isa. 14:7, 9); that would be Forsakenness. YHWH is the Liberator, he creates salvation, i.e., the room to live before his face. But thus YHWH also makes the earth into a land of the living (Ps. 27:13; Isa. 38:11) by creating freedom for the disenfranchised and the enslaved. He has—and this is the driving force in world history—[116] a dispute with rulers who violate justice (Isa. 11:4; Ezek. 34:22).

God is a judge of the nations. That does not mean that he speaks judgment in the first instance, but he provides them with justice (Judg. 6:14,15; 8:22,23; 1 Sam. 8:5,6,20; 1 Sam. 11:13). God will be King. That means: when he through his liberation has put the powers-of-the-deep in their place, he will have led history to peace, just as he established and ordained nature in the beginning. "And he saw that it was good" (Gen. 1:31; Rev. 21:5). The name Jesus, *Yehoshua*, means Liberator, for he shall give his people knowledge of their liberation through the forgiveness of their sins (Luke 1:77). "Stand then in the freedom with which Christ has made us free" (Gal. 5:1). "You are sealed to the day of liberation" (Eph. 4:30). To this end do we see the way of God going. That is how we, by faith, understand history.

-10-

But, pay attention: the sacred teaching also speaks in a different manner about "God's Way," namely, as *synonymous with: the fulfilment of God's commandments*. "Lord, make me to know your ways:" (Ps. 25:4), i.e. the ways which I must walk in to be pleasing to you. They are then not my ways in the first place, though they are my acts. And if they are called "God's ways," they are not unconnected to God's Way in the above-mentioned sense: of the course which strives in and against and to the end of history, they signify a *participation* in the Means to fulfilment.

"He will teach the humble his way" (Ps. 25:9b). "Teach me your way, O Lord; I will walk in your truth; unite my heart to the fear of your Name." (Ps. 86:11) "I delight in the way of your testimonies more than in riches." (Ps. 119:114) "They have not known my ways" (Heb. 3:10 cited from Psalm 95).

In the book of Acts "the way of the Lord" comes to mean the teaching, i.e., the proclamation of Christ, the life of the congregation of Christ, in short, as we might say: *Christendom* (if we may still use this word without creating misunderstanding), as human history.

Acts 18:25 says about Apollos that he was taught in the way of the Lord (n.b. "only knowing of the baptism of John")—but when Aquila and Priscilla heard him, they drew to him and explained to him [117] the *way of God* deeper and more precisely. And Saul persecutes those who were "of that way" (i.e. of that faith, of that sect), Acts 9:2—and in Ephesus the synagogues begin to speak evil "of the way" (Acts 19:9); later no small stir begins "because of the way" (19:23), the way of life. The way, that is: holy history as God's history; corresponding to that, and related mysteriously to it, . . . is "our way," i.e., the way of confession and action of the congregation, unobtrusive and thwarted in the world, yet authentic.

It could not possibly be the same word by accident; God's Way and our way agree. If God's Way is ultimately described by verbal forms (in the Apostles' Creed): conceived, born, suffered, crucified, died, buried, *descended—raised*, ascended, sitting, coming—then "our way" will describe the same course: from the "state of humiliation" to the "state of exaltation," a suffering and a doing, according to the measure of humanity.

"Therefore we are always of good courage" (2 Cor. 5:6,8). For thus it will be with all of creation: humbled, exalted!

Holy history encloses world history! Because it reveals, as the breaking through of the "eternal return," the trackless event, the cycle of things, YHWH as the deity, and his deity in his attributes, and in his noble way.

We need to get back briefly to the concept of holy history. That term does not mean world history as such, neither is church history the arena of God's acts, still less is nature in the way it functions. Thus the Old Testament has *different* words for the "works" of God in creation and for his "acts" in history, where he establishes a memorial for his Name. The particular Hebrew word for "act" means that God's inclination turns inside out, so that he may be known and recognized by his "act," very differently than in his "works."

At special times it appears that his heart perseveres in this or that act of help and deliverance. At such times *intention* and *act* are not only close together, but identical. He is "great in counsel and mighty (busy in the act) in deed" (Jer. 32:19). That is a parallel, because they are synonymous.

In the *works* one *cannot* meet God, in history only here and there an event may be qualified as his act. People who say: "God is all" or "God wills all" or "God does [118] all," speak about someone else; they misunderstand the Name, cancel the idea of his virtues and, because they speak so generally and thoughtlessly, they disturb the salutary knowledge of his way. In addition, they postulate a continuity, which simply cannot be visible to us. We can only speak of "Way," insofar as there is a relationship between the one qualified moment and the other. For the acts of God intend the freedom of the creature, place his goodness in the light, his resistance to all tyrants, and the deliverances he gives to all who are suppressed. God's acts are the footsteps of the Anointed (Ps. 89:52; Ps. 85:14). He is the Pioneer, the King, the Leader, whose footsteps one can and may follow (Exod. 11:8; 1 Kings 20:10) into the kingdom where "steadfast love and faithfulness will meet, righteousness and peace will kiss each other" (Ps. 85:11). Thus, he distinguishes himself *in* the world *from* the world, thus he sets himself apart against all that happens and all that is done in world history and not infrequently man does not notice it (Ps. 77:20).

Appendix C: "The Election of Israel"

K. H. Miskotte
De kern van de zaak

Toelichting bij een proeve van hernieuwd belijden (Nijkerk: G. F. Callenbach, 1950)

Private Translation by Martin Kessler

But God, who does not give his honor to another and who does not desire that the sinner should die but that he repent and live, does not abandon the work of his hands but holds fast to his kingship. Therefore, in the midst of peoples estranged from him, in Israel he has chosen and called a people, that it might be to him a priestly kingdom and a holy nation, that it might experience that salvation and peace of humanity are found in living by God's royal favor and law. Thus, in Israel's law, sacrificial service, and kingship, God has granted a prophecy of his coming kingdom, of his intentions for the whole earth.

But the people of God has not understood this ordering of God's grace, as is witnessed already by the Old Testament. Israel has sought its salvation with the powers of the earth or with its own piety and works. Thus, Israel has not received the promise, but has become disgraced again and again under God's judgments.

Nevertheless, the chosen people has had to serve the plans of God even in its unbelief. It is set up as a mirror in which we see ourselves, as a sign of the unwillingness and lack of power of all men to live by God's power and grace.

—Article 3, *Fundamenten en perspectieven van belijden* (A Proposed New Confession for the Dutch Reformed Church)

I. Compared to older confessional documents, this article adds a new element: Israel. This is a result of:

a) A more historical understanding of revelation;
b) A point of orientation forced on us by recent history;

check p. 355 of Barth on Romans (in ed. at Sem), Imp. for (Unwritten letters)

c) A clearer insight into the secret of Israel's election as pars pro toto, [43] representative; also as example and pledge, as preaching and admonition. There will hardly be anyone—at least in the church—who has not been strengthened by "anti-Semitism" in the realization that Israel represents a very particular secret. From that follows indeed a series of new (or old and forgotten) accents, namely that God meets us in *history*, that history is a weaving of grace and judgment, that the elect bear the heaviest burden in this world, still made heavier when they forget their own election; that whatever *happens to us* individually, *is experienced* collectively, spiritually, and physically—that in the midst of, and in spite of catastrophic estrangements, God remains faithful to his people. These insights have caused better preaching and simpler care of souls: the super-spiritual, the pietistic, the heaven-oriented, the unworldly and nonpolitical is replaced by more biblical notions. One notes a general receding of religious idealism. Life has become rougher, the thunder of world events has drowned out the organ of the conventicle [symbolizing sentimental worship]. The majesty and wrath, the judgments and liberations of the God who goes his awesome way from of old, right through the drama of history, have touched many. Surely this situation [gesteltenis] may unjustly overshadow other things. However, that does not mean that what we (re)discover later is diminished compared to what we here confess. Both are totally valid; no synthesis is gained by detracting anything from either side. We need to guard against drawing hasty conclusions, however. For this movement of motives brings *dangers* with it also; there is presently a tendency by some to replace the faith that the Holy Scriptures are the Word of God, by the faith that Israel is God's people. This is a dangerous turn which threatens right confessing. One may then be embarrassed by the study of Scripture that is both spiritual and scientific, [44] one may fear an abstract theology and flee to the ordinary stuff of history, as it indeed persists among us, as "sacred" history, in the existence of Israel. We must not go in that direction. We do not live by history, but by the Word, we do not stand in the stream of history without standing under the power of the Spirit. We must not change from idealism to a realism which binds God to what exists, to the event, to the fact, to power. Meanwhile this bad option is not necessarily related to the thrust intended here, as appears clearly enough from this article.

II. However, the great merit of this new approach lies in this, that the confession of God's kingship and man's rebellion (both are a confession of faith!) leads to the confession of the *election* of Israel. What the church means by the vocable "God" is thus drawn away powerfully from the broad and fine considerations concerning his being; what the church confesses by the term "sin" is thus transferred into a different sphere from the one in which one is still pastorally preoccupied with "man" and searches for the remnants of the divine image.

God and man are related. Who God is, is revealed in this, that the destiny of man is maintained . . . , but also in that the *relationship on his part* continues, that he "does not abandon the work of his hands." How are God and man mutually related? We do not know how it was in paradise; how it is now, in this world, we know, but we do not see any meaning in it. But we see in *Israel,* (i.e., in the light of the Word) how God and man are related. That is the subject presently, that we view God's "being" and man's "being" together in the election of Israel.

[45] III. Ultimately, everything becomes salvifically clear in the election of Jesus Christ (which in our view *precedes* Israel's election and must therefore be confessed first), while the election of Israel is but an image and application of the election of Jesus Christ and his body (the church). If one wished to express this, then this entire confession would have to be conceived less on the level of history and historical sequence and less horizontally, and there would be more reckoning with the vertical dimension from the beginning: the dimension of Decision, of Eternity, of the permanence in God's pleasure. However, the fullness of the truth does not only permit but *demand* that we approach and describe it in various ways. In this way we come to view yet another context, which can help us along the way, to confess more broadly and happily, more concretely and widely.

IV. God has "*in the midst of* the people *estranged* from him," *chosen* and *called* a people in Israel . . . this is entirely historical, salfivic-historical, yet historically conceived. It is as infralapsarian as possible , i.e., it presupposes apostasy, disobedience, rebellion, the estrangement of man—and on that basis election begins. Such estrangement is therefore not conceived as a result of God's eternal election and rejection [which would be supralapsarian].

Indeed, this is our first impression in the Bible. Suddenly, there is Abraham, not indigenous, not autochthon, but called away and set apart. An entire people arises which, with all its folly [onbenul] and recalcitrance, is related to God. See, there is a covenant; begun *from one side,* so that it might become *bilateral,* a living relationship of spirit with spirit, heart with heart, act of God with human act, word with answer. Thus, the kingdom began to press on the world. We will not easily be cured of speculation and abstraction [46] if we do not learn to see the typically divine action in election, which makes its trajectory in history. It would not be impossible to derive from the election of Israel everything which has been written up in many volumes on the attributes of God, and what in later times was taught about anthropology. To derive? No, it jumps out at us as soon as we look for it there. Thus is God, so is man; all ages concern themselves with the relationship between this God and this man. Further, what sin is appears here in the true light: the unfaithfulness, the refusal to live for him, who has become our life. We suspect already that the faith, which the church is encouraged to hold, cannot be any other than the faith in him who "justifies the ungodly." (Rom. 4:5)

V. The destiny of man in general is evident in the *special* destiny of Israel. The particularity of Israel is hidden in its destiny, not to be anything special in itself, but in *man in general* as object of God's grace. Man as such, who is estranged from his origin, is neither good nor bad in a moral sense; he is wrong, but he does not repent; such is man! But God *turns* to him, God chooses him. He chooses in himself solicitude rather than indifference, keeping rather than allowing-to-be-lost; he chooses as king, i.e., in *his* royal manner, in the manner of royal grace, which is indeed free, but bound to *his* nature-of-freedom, far removed from any caprice. For he reveals himself as the *faithful one,* who desires not death but life, not destruction but salvation. He does not reveal himself in mixed forms, in ambiguities, in halfheartedness. He is not a little kind and a little angry. He is totally just and totally gracious. Living thus "he maintains his kingship," [47] he, the electing God, reveals himself in that manner, according to his character, according to which "he has his own reasons" to do what no one has asked him or would dare to ask him to do.

VI. *Election and destiny! They belong together,* they are obverse and reverse! What then will be the destiny of Israel? The answer to that question is bound to our confession about the future of "man in general." We are not speaking of distant things; this refers to ourselves! "That it might be to him a *priestly kingdom* and a *holy people.*" Conceiving election first of all individually, and relating it primarily to the goal of "salvation"—that is the double burden that often precludes our understanding of the salvific message. Election relates to Christ and his *people.* If one wishes to abstract provisionally from Christ (a rather strange work for the Christian congregation), then election relates to the people, the congregation, the living, working, suffering community, the army, the battle array, the pioneers, the martyrs in their unity with the King and with each other. Election pertains primarily to a people, a multitude of people, more in their activity than in their essence, their actively and passively being busy, their working-differently, suffering-differently, hoping-differently from what is characteristic about the "wrong" man. This is about the super-individual.

About the second point: in the mirror of Israel we see clearly that destiny is not salvation but *holiness.* That remains valid when we understand "holiness" in its biblical sense, i.e., not morally or idealistically. Holy means to be dedicated to God by its relationship: a holy day, a holy place, a holy vessel, a holy people. It is a long road, which many have so often struggled over, to move from election to the good life; [48] it appears to be an illusion. Election *itself* is being committed to holiness. One must not measure any distance here, nor seek to cross, for this is only present in the being-commited as such. Election *leads* directly *to ethics,* it is being privileged to holiness, to being different and to live differently, and therefore to live rightly, simply, originally, purely. . . .

However, this "ethics" is essentially not morality, nor a codex of prescriptions. Israel is chosen that it "might experience that *salvation* [heil] and *peace* for mankind is found in living by God's royal favor and law."

We may experience something! What living really is, finally to live . . . what all pagans hanker after.

By God's favor and by his law. Favor comes first, for the law itself is a gift of grace. We do not live "according to" the law, but rather *by* the law, through the "Torah," the teaching, which directs our steps on the way. In that life lies salvation and peace for (all) mankind. Again, salvation first, while peace, shalom, is the wellbeing which flows from order, which in turn originates from the fact that all things are "in order" [alright!] between the king and his people.

VII. The *prophetic, priestly, and royal office,* to which man is destined (the content of man as "holy," being-different) was granted by God to Israel. It was portrayed in the *figures* [gestalten] of lawgiver and prophet, in the priest, in the king; or rather, it was imaged and became present in this image itself, whereby the lawgiver as a person merges in the *event* [happening] of the law, of instruction, of preaching, the priest in offering and praise, and the king in his manner of reigning, speaking justice, and leading. (In Christology, we need to avoid every separation of person and office.)

[49] When we have "the election of Israel" as article of faith (the 19th century has injected into our bloodstream the subjectivization of everything!) some might think that we choose the "religion of Israel" above pagan religion: to defend its quality, to propagate and spiritualize it. However, we are concerned with what God has done in his royal activity, not with right or wrong human religions; whether they are apostate or have originated through prophetic renewal—there is for us no binding authority in the religion of exemplary people or their opposite: horribly ungrateful people. "The eyes keep our quiet mind directed upward, to pay attention to God" (Psalm 25 : 6 rhymed). The concern is with God, and with his faithfulness in governing, when we regard the three holy offices and and see them at work, the concern is with this God in his exceptional being-busy with the stubborn material of the "holy" people.

VIII. All of this in its exceptionality remains a sign and promise "for the *whole earth,*" says the article.

God himself is *present* in Torah and sacrifice and royal service. He is somewhere—not everywhere-and-nowhere. He "is," i.e., he deals with us, as with the earth, that the earth might be full of the knowledge of the Lord (Isa. 11 : 9).

Man lives in proximity to God through obedience, surrender, and glorifying him, thereby representing earth and mankind.

The meaning of man's existence is revealed and fulfilled in election and destiny, God's election and man's destiny, when they are joined. The Kingdom has come; reality is justified, salvation is valid and active, joy has opened up forever and ever. However . . .

[50] IX. Again: "*however.*" Essentially this turn is not a different turn from man's rebellion. This is hardly an imaginary repetition, but rather a confirmation of the inner impossibility and feared reality of sin. "*Impossible*" insofar as God's creation, i.e., his being-busy-creatively, excludes sin; "*really*" insofar as our reality apparently contains also an uncreated side or a fringe, which God rejects as a possibility in his continuous, good creation. Thus, Israel's calling and deliverance out of Egypt, all of the signs and wonders on its journey through the wilderness, were also a good, an abundantly good work. God is king, our king also in that he does not abandon the work that his hand began with us. It is hoped that no one regards this as a pious turn of phrase; this rather concerns the only grounds for the continued existence of the world, for the defense against radical chaos, for life that triumphs from the rubble. It is also the only ground for the existence of Israel—miniature humanity—particularly blessed and burdened, the church in embryo, borne in grace and struggling again and again with their own aversion against all the grace it receives.

What has happened then? Israel did not understand its being together with God, this paradise in the midst of all adventures, as *grace*. It wanted to be a creating *partner* itself, it wanted to *use* God to become pious and great; and finally it preferred to be *alone* and excused from the "burden" of its election; it wanted to be like other people in all respects, and nevertheless to be apart and to maintain the pretense of keeping the name of "God's people." "That cannot be"—but it is!

"This story is told about *you.*" For that reason the "election of Israel" belongs in the confession of the church. Thus, we confess our faith and our *guilt.* We place ourselves [51] in solidarity with this strange, audacious behavior; we admit that our estrangement (after we are called and chosen in the church) and our most impenetrable *ingratitude* crop out. We are horrible to look at in our bewilderment, pathetic in our loneliness, disgusting in our pretense and yet, in spite of all, "holy," different from the "world" and the "heathen." We are unintelligible in our unbelief. By confessing the election of Israel, the church pronounces the severest judgment on itself, on the immense hypocrisy that accompanies all human piety, on the unbridled tyranny which joins all human morality, on the hardness of its heart, the stiffness of its neck, the lovelessness of its behavior, the despicability of its religious egoism, the lack of apostolic fervor, the failure, it seems, of everything, of everything that we touch.

When someone still asks why in this confessional writing Israel is introduced near the beginning, appearing to eclipse the old preliminary articles—wouldn't we then finally have to answer: because we were permitted to leave the forecourt of philosophy to find ourselves again in the biblical world with the *indicated forecourt:* the Old Testament (not as deposit of Israel's religion, but as witness of the royal faithfulness of Israel's God). And doesn't this order commend itself? What does the book in every pulpit of our church look like? Will we as a congregation find ourselves counterfeited in the first part? Yet don't we know that in this self-recognition and acknowledgment we truly begin to be a congregation for the first time? We must and we may be in solidarity with Israel. "For there is no difference; all have sinned and fallen short of the glory of God but are justified freely (by the redemption which is in Christ Jesus, Rom. 3:23).

[52] X. "*Nevertheless* the chosen people has also had to *serve* God's plan in its unbelief."

A new dimension of God's kingship is here introduced. . . . What we do is in vain and what we intend is ridiculous. "*In vain*" is not pessimistically intended here; neither is "ridiculous" meant to sound destructive. Israel is a raised sign of that also: how much in vain, and how ridiculous—and yet, even this is preparatory for a deeper intention and a better covenant. Now our failure becomes useful to us.

A higher and more gracious wisdom invalidates our wrong track. If we would succeed in our doing, we would lapse into eternal death; blessed and promising laughter cuts through our intentions; if we were left alone with whatever excites us while we conjure up our fantastic plans, we would already be incurably insane. *However!* This is the great "however," measured to which our "howevers" and Israel's "howevers" appear so trivial and innocent. That is *the divine turning*, which embraces our "turning-away" with arms of blessing.

XI. In all of its bitter reality, Israel is yet only a "mirror" in which we see ourselves, our unwillingness and lack of power. With this word "*mirror*" reality is not evaporated but relativized; it only appears as evaporated. Everything becomes "relative" by what is posited *over against it* by God, namely the firm, unshakable *resolve* to establish and share salvation over all the earth, for people who had become "impossible," because of the life that had become "in vain" and the striving that had become "ridiculous."

This firm, unshakable resolve is already behind this entire activity. . . . [53] In Jesus Christ the holy people will appear complete on earth, and enter history. In him the destiny of man will be fulfilled as the election of God. In him God is manifest as the true God, and in him man is manifest as true man. In him is the holy, the totally-different, the most-general: your righteousness and mine. In him Israel's privilege will be shared by all peoples. And the kingdom of God will be established among us, never to disappear. That is the goal and end of all failure. Here every "yes-but" of unbelief is *endlessly* eclipsed by the But and the Yes! of God. Therefore the Christian, with all madness and misery, remains repentant and homesick, but without tragic consciousness. And the greatest thing that may be said about Israel, remains this: in all of its sorrow it is *not* tragic. This also is a reflection [weerglans] of its election.

Notes

Chapter 1. Miskotte the Man

1. *Wenn die Götter schweigen: Vom Sinn des Alten Testaments.* (Munich: Chr. Kaiser, 1963; third printing, 1966); translated by H. Stoevesandt from *Als de goden zwijgen* [When the Gods are Silent] (Amsterdam: Uitgeversmaatschappij Holland, 1956; second printing 1965 and reprinted in Verzameld Werk [Collected Work] 8). The German edition is a revised version of the Dutch original.

2. *When the Gods are Silent.* Translated by John W. Doberstein (New York/Evanston: Harper and Row, 1967). See n.1.

3. "This is a book of theology, fundamentally concerned with preaching and expounding Christian faith. As an entrance to the most recent era of European Protestant theology, the book would be valuable for the undergraduate were it not so specifically focused on the Old Testament." *Choice* 5 (November 1968), 1150. Another reviewer writes: "Mr. Miskotte . . . has a difficult style of writing . . . [He] speaks to his peers; therefore the work challenges the reader's knowledge of theology and historical exegesis." *Library Journal* 92 (Oct. 15, 1967), 3646.

4. Abraham Kuyper (1837–1920), Dutch theologian, is briefly described, very likely because his Princeton Stone Lectures were published in England in 1932. See n.8, Chap. 2.

5. H. Stoevesandt, editor of *Karl Barth –Kornelis Heiko Miskotte Briefwechsel 1924–1968* (Zurich: Theologisches Verlag, 1991), gives the following list (almost all of them he himself translated): *Zur biblischen Hermeneutik.* Theologische Studien, 55 (Zollikon: Evangelischer Verlag, 1959); *Über Karl Barths Kirchliche Dogmatik: Kleine Präludien und Phantasien,* Theologische Existenz heute, Neue Folge Heft 89 (1961); *Der Weg des Gebets* (Munich: Chr. Kaiser, 1964); *Biblische Meditationen.* (Munich: Chr. Kaiser, 1967); *Predigten aus vier Jahrzehnten* (Munich: Chr. Kaiser, 1969); *Das Judentum als Frage an die Kirche* (Wuppertal, 1970); *Der Gott Israels und die Theologie: Ausgewählte Aufsätze* (Neukirchen: Neukirchener Verlag, 1975); *Biblisches ABC: Wider das unbiblische Bibellesen* (Neukirchen: Neukirchener Verlag, 1976).

6. Among recent dissertations submitted to the Rijksuniversiteit, Utrecht, dealing with Miskotte are: G. G. de Kruijf, *Heiden, Jood en Christen: Een studie over de theologie van K. H. Miskotte* [Pagan, Jew and Christian: A Study of the Theology of K. H. Miskotte] (Baarn: Ten Have, 1981); Marinus J. G. van der Velden, *K. H. Miskotte als prediker: Een homiletisch onderzoek* [K. H. Miskotte the Preacher: A Homiletical Study] (The Hague: Boekencentrum, 1984); Jan Muis, *Openbaring en Interpretatie: Het verstaan van de Heilige Schrift volgens K. Barth en K. H. Miskotte* [Revelation and Interpretation: The Understanding of Holy Scripture according to K. Barth and K. H. Miskotte] (The Hague: Boekencentrum, 1989).

7. Every fall semester, one of Miskotte's works is chosen for study by a group of theological students at the University of Amsterdam.

8. According to Professor H. H. Miskotte, courtesy Mrs. E. Kuiper-Miskotte (a daughter of Prof. Miskotte).

9. Two concise biographical resources are: H. C. Touw, "Prof. dr. K. H. Miskotte. Zijn weg in Woord en wereld." In *Woord en Wereld. Opgedragen aan Prof. Dr. K. H. Miskotte naar aanleiding van zijn aftreden als kerkelijk hoogleraar te Leiden op 14 december 1959* [Word and World. Dedicated to Prof. Dr. K. H. Miskotte on the Occasion of his Retirement as Ecclesiastical Professor, Leiden, December 14, 1959] (Amsterdam: Arbeiderspers, 1961), 9–75, and H. H. Miskotte, *Niet te vergeten Miskotte* [Miskotte not to be forgotten] (Kampen: J. H. Kok, 1981).

10. R. Zuurmond, "Twee voetnoten bij K. H. Miskotte's Theologie van het Oude Testament [Two Footnotes to K. H. Miskotte's Theology of the Old Testament]," in K. H. Miskotte, *De weg der verwachting* [The Way of Expectation] (Baarn: Ten Have, 1975), 24.

11. K. A. Deurloo, "Ter inleiding. Hij schrijft ons een teken van leven [Introduction. He Writes us a Sign of Life]," *De weg der verwachting*, 7.

12. In a letter dated July 12, 1956, Barth wrote to Miskotte: "Lieber Heiko, du bist der Seher und Dichter unter meinen Freunden!" *Briefwechsel*, 81.

13. Mrs. E. Kuiper-Miskotte writes: "His diary betrays an overwhelming variety of topics from the mystical to the activist" but also makes the point that Miskotte's theological development cannot be followed through his diaries. She claims that a better picture may be had from the *Briefwechsel*, selections of which are translated in Verzameld Werk 2: K. H. Miskotte, Karl Barth, *Inspiratie en vertolking: inleidingen, essays, briefwisseling* [Inspiration and Interpretation: Introductions, Essays, Correspondence], eds. A. Geense and H. Stoevesandt. (Kampen: J. H. Kok, 1987). Thus far, two volumes of the diaries have been published: *Uit de dagboeken 1917–1930*, Verzameld Werk 4 [From the Diaries 1917–1930. Collected Work 4], eds. E. Kuiper-Miskotte, H. H. Miskotte (Kampen: J. H. Kok, 1985) and *Uit de dagboeken 1930–1934*. Verzameld werk 5A (Kampen: J. H. Kok, 1990). It was originally planned that the diaries should take up only two volumes in the Collected Works, but there is still far more material that might be published. The third volume of the diaries will cover the period from 1935 through the end of the war (according to Mrs. E. Kuiper-Miskotte). It is scheduled for publication in 1996.

14. In an article entitled "De beteekenis der catechesatie [The Significance of Catechizing]," in *In de gecroonde allemansgading: Keur uit het verspreide werk van Prof. Dr K. H. Miskotte* [Celebration Volume: Selections from the Scattered Works of Prof. Dr. K. H. Miskotte], eds. W. C. Snethlage, E. A. J. Plug. (Nijkerk: G. F. Callenbach, 1946, second printing). Miskotte singles out Dr. J. R. Slotemaker de Bruïne, Utrecht pastor, who taught him catechism for more than 7 years: " . . . what I have profited from him cannot be said in a few words, but [I can testify to] the profound impression he made on me: [he was] an exemplary catechist; one noticed that he deemed catechetical training at least as important as the sermon, one could feel how he had prepared himself spiritually; he taught according to our capacity for understanding . . . He gave himself so much to this work, so that it . . . entered the homes, the parents noted . . . that something special was going on." (255, 256)

15. Specifically B. J. H. Ovink (philosopher), H. Th. Obbink (historian of religion) and Hugo Visscher (philosopher). His Old Testament professor was A. H. Edelkoort (1890–1956). Miskotte found him to be on a vastly different wavelength from his own. Later, after hearing a lecture by him concerning the pastorate, Mis-

kotte spoke of his "bourgeois virtue and farmer's logic" being joined together (*Dagboeken 1930–1934,* 271). See chap. 2, n.12.

16. Especially his little book *Die Lehre des Heils* (Elberfeld, 1903) which Miskotte urged Karl Barth to read, in an early communication (*Briefwechsel,* 15). In fact, it appears that Miskotte one time had intended to write his dissertation on the doctrine of sanctification in the preaching of H. F. Kohlbrügge. See chap. 2.

17. See chap. 2, "Influence of Karl Barth."

18. His son (Prof. Dr. H. H. Miskotte, University of Amsterdam) writes that Miskotte's library had a division for philosophy and theology, and one on art and history, with a large division of Dutch literature; also English and French, but particularly German literature. His theological books were not more than half of his library (*Niet te vergeten Miskotte,* 98, 99).

19. Niet te vergeten Miskotte, 102.

20. In his published diaries, see n.13 above.

21. K. H. Miskotte, . . . *als een die dient: volledige uitgave van het 'Gemeenteblaadje Cortgene'* [. . . as one who serves: Complete Edition of the 'Cortgene Parish Paper'] (Baarn: Ten Have, 1982, second printing).

22. In a desperate letter while serving in Meppel (dated April 8, 1929), breathing a de profundis atmosphere, Miskotte wrote to Barth that the day before, in a service where he preached on Question and Answer 44 of the *Heidelberg Catechism* [on the Creed, the "descent to hell"], he announced to the congregation that he could not preach, that they would pray and sing and go home. In his words: "The tensions in the last years in this half-methodistic, half liberal congregation, brought a sudden derailment [Entgleisung], which no one could understand. . . . I was suddenly without contact with people and without contact from above [nach oben], in a fearful emptiness in which every word and gesture appeared senseless to me. . . ." He asked Barth for comfort and whether he should resign his call because of this experience (*Briefwechsel,* 21).

23. Mrs. E. Kuiper-Miskotte writes in her "Introduction" to the first of the published diaries that Haarlem was a much more hospitable place (compared to his first two congregations). "The Great or Bavo Church [in Haarlem] elevated his spirit. His congregation was more sympathetic . . . and he made friends" (*Dagboeken 1917–1930,* 6).

24. *Woord en Wereld,* 22, 23. See n.9 above.

25. While serving his Meppel pastorate, he wrote in his diary: "The book of Ruth is much more profound than is usually thought" (*Dagboeken 1917–1930,* October 17, 1926 entry). His studies on Ruth were published as: *Het gewone leven: In den spiegel van het boek Ruth* [The Common Life: In the Mirror of the Book of Ruth] (Amsterdam: Uitgeversmaatschappij Holland, 1939). His study on Job was entitled *Antwoord uit het onweer: Een verhandeling over het boek Job* [Answer out of the Storm: A Discourse on the book of Job]. Revised second edition of *De verborgene* [The Hidden One] (Amsterdam: Uitgeversmaatschappij Holland, 1936). Both works are reprinted in Verzameld Werk 10 (Kampen: J. H. Kok, 1984). The genesis of his work on Job was in his Cortgene parish where in his newsletter he had dealt with Job and the problem of suffering.

26. *Het Wezen der Joodse Religie* (Amsterdam: Paris, 1932. Second printing, Haarlem: Uitgeversmaatschappij Holland, 1964).

27. Abel J. Herzberg wrote that "during the occupation, it was for many Jews a source of strength in all sorrow" (Quoted in *Niet te vergeten Miskotte,* 155). His dissertation is discussed in chap. 3.

28. *Edda en Thora* (Nijkerk: G. F. Callenbach, 1939; second printing, 1970.

Reprinted in Verzameld Werk 7. Kampen: J. H. Kok, 1983). The title had many people puzzled: some thought that it might be a book about the pastor's two daughters (H. C. Touw, "Prof. Dr. K. H. Miskotte. Zijn Weg in Woord en Wereld," *Woord en Wereld,* 35. Appendix A of the present work contains a translation of chapter 1 of *Edda en Thora.*

29. Reprinted in: *Gecroonde allemansgading,* 287–294. It opens with the moving words: "Since the German strategic 'occupation' has exposed itself as an excuse to nazify the Netherlands, our good, free Netherlands, with the violation of our history, with contempt for the convictions of our people, the resistance among our people has increased hand over fist."

30. *Bijbels ABC* [Biblical ABCs]. (Nijkerk: G. F. Callenbach, 1941. Seventh printing, Baarn: Ten Have, 1992). This book is also translated in German (see n.5 above) and in Italian: *ABC della Bibbia* (Brescia, 1981).

31. *Dienstboek voor de Nederlandse Hervormde Kerk* [Service Book for the Dutch Reformed Church] (The Hague: Boekencentrum, 1957), 303–305.

32. Miskotte had always had socialist leanings, as did Karl Barth, his teacher. In his first parish, Miskotte was sometimes called "red pastor." Among the Protestant political parties before World War II, the most powerful was the Anti-Revolutionary Party, which was founded on the (Neo-Calvinist) teachings of Abraham Kuyper who posited an "antithesis" in society, based on Christian faith. Before the war, the (larger) Roman Catholic Party joined in a coalition with the Protestant parties (which made for a politically conservative government). In the document explaining the pastors' action, we read: "It is our conviction that we might render church and people a great service, if we would surrender the antithesis-thought, which estranges the church from the practical relationships of real life and keeps the people at a distance from trust in the supra-party concerns of the outreach of the gospel . . . [However], no single party, not even one labeled 'Christian' can be a spiritual home for a Christian. *Our home is the church; the S.D.A.P. is for us no more than a temporary political camp in which we may work with others for the realization of a practical political and social program* (Quoted from Touw, "Prof. Dr. K. H. Miskotte," 47–48, italics added).

33. In a letter dated August 31, 1945, he wrote to Barth (about his Leiden appointment): "It will not be simple to function in such an autonomous milieu, equipped with such a poor deposit of ready scholarship, as a 50 year old Pastor after 25 years of service (mostly in a large city) can muster. The faculty unanimously and emphatically rejected me. [But] the Synod has gone its own way." (*Briefwechsel,* 62)

34. Touw, "*Prof. dr. K. H. Miskotte,*" 49.

35. Ibid., 50.

36. Ibid., 52.

37. *Liedboek voor de kerken* [Song Book for the Churches] (The Hague: Boekencentrum & Leeuwarden: Jongbloed, 1978)

38. This is the original (Dutch) edition which was expanded, revised, and translated into German: *Wenn die Götter schweigen* which became the basis for the English edition: *When the Gods are Silent.* See n. 2.

39. *When the Gods are Silent,* 1.

40. Touw, "Prof. dr. K. H. Miskotte," 57.

41. *Om het Levende Woord* (The Hague: Daamen, 1948. Second printing, Kampen: J. H. Kok, 1973).

42. *Briefwechsel,* 9–10.

43. See n.6, chap. 1.

44. Otto Weber (1902–1966) wrote about the Dutch original of *When the Gods are Silent:* "Your book is written in such a hieratic language, that it is untranslatable." (Cited in a letter from Miskotte to Barth, May 7, 1958, in *Briefwechsel,* 118). This may be partly the reason why his magnum opus was not very enthusiastically received in the English-speaking world. But the major reason is likely the fact that Miskotte was ahead of the American philosophical discussion. It is hoped that his work may have another chance, as interest in Miskotte is experiencing some kind of revival (in Europe at least).

Chapter 2. On the Sources of His Thought

1. See n.14, chap. 1.

2. A fruitful source for tracing Miskotte's intellectual history is *Briefwechsel* See n.5, chap. 1.

3. His interest in Gunning went back to his Cortgene days, where he contributed a number of articles to the works on Gunning. See chap. 2, introductory comments.

4. Among his Bible studies we have (in addition to his works on Ruth and Job, see n.25, chap. 1): *De profeet Elija: Gelijkenissen van het Godsrijk, en de Openbaring van Johannes* [The Prophet Elijah: Parables of the Kingdom of God, and The Revelation of John]—transcribed Bible studies during his Amsterdam pastorate. Also *Hoofdsom der historie: Voordrachten over de visioenen van den apostel Johannes* [Summation of History: Lectures on the Visions of the Apostle John] (Nijkerk: G. F. Callenbach, 1945). His studies on Ruth (see n.25, chap. 1) have been considered his finest work on any part of the Bible.

5. Another Zeitspiegel which he wrote (based on lectures at Delft) is "Het geestesmerk van de europese mens en het Evangelie van Jezus Christus [The Spiritual Marks of European Man and the Gospel of Jesus Christ]" in Dr. K. H. Miskotte, *Grensgebied* [Borderland] (Nijkerk: G. F. Callenbach, 1954?), 9–51.

6. All of this underscores the complexity of the man. Some have wondered aloud: Will the time ever arrive when we may write the biography of Miskotte? (de Kruijf, *Heiden, Jood en Christen,* 12). In this chapter the best we can do is to offer some comments illustrating how multifaceted were his interests, and how wide his reading.

7. This choice would seem eminently logical, in view of his life-long interest in Gunning, whose writings influenced him greatly. See his *Johannes Hermanus Gunning* (Rotterdam: 1941).

8. This refers to the theology of Abraham Kuyper (1837–1920), who engineered a church split in 1886 in the Dutch Reformed Church, and subsequently, a reunion with an earlier secession (dating from 1834). Kuyper was a formidable theologian; he delivered the Stone Lectures at Princeton Seminary in 1898, which were published in England in 1932 under the title *Calvinism.* He also served as a member of the Dutch Parliament. The theology of the church he established: Gereformeerde Kerken in Nederland, which has been labeled "neo-Calvinist." See Miskotte, "Korte nabetrachting over de Afscheiding van 1834 [Brief Reflection on the Secession of 1834]" in K. H. Miskotte, *Om de waarheid te zeggen: Opstellen over het kerkelijk belijden* [To Tell the Truth: Essays concerning Church Confession]. (Kampen: J. H. Kok, 1971), 13–57, and "Kanttekeningen bij het gedenkboek der Doleantie [Marginal Notes with the Memorial Book of the (Church Division of 1886)], ibid., 58–86.

9. Since a vast portion of his reading moved in the area of literature and culture, one would think that this would have been a very suitable choice.
10. A favorite Flemish poet (1830–99).
11. Diary entry, January 10, 1919.
12. On December 9, 1926, he wrote: "Edelkoort is still the same intelligent bourgeois boy, but still more sober than before." There are several additional entries, seldom very positive. In his diary for March 21, 1927, he wrote about a visit to Edelkoort; Miskotte told him that he appreciated his scientific honesty (referring to biblical criticism). He wrote in his diary: "[Edelkoort displays] . . . a certain bourgeois attention to little, good things in life—but [he represents] my 'antipode' in religion. [Even] God himself is a citizen for him . . . 'Ethical' is morality minus the mystical. And all of this annoyingly consistent."
13. This is discussed in some detail in "Removing the Rubbish" (*When the Gods are Silent*, 61–65) which is a direct attack on common misconceptions about the Bible, of which, felt Miskotte, misguided people are so sure. The worst of them is about God.
14. H. H. Miskotte, *Niet te Vergeten Miskotte*, 102.
15. See n.6, chap. 1.
16. In the words of Muis: "In the Netherlands we have learned to read and appreciate Barth via Miskotte; for many the work of Barth and Miskotte forms 'wirkungsgeschichtlich' and materially a unity." But as Muis also shows, the situation is much more complicated than a simple master-disciple relationship. Even so, there is no question that Miskotte all his life regarded Barth as his theological father (*Openbaring*, 15). Paradoxically, on the one hand Miskotte must be seen as an original thinker with unique insights but on the other hand as a Barth-interpreter who liked nothing better than that Barth's works were read and appropriated (*Openbaring*, 359).
17. Muis, *Openbaring*, 358.
18. Ibid.
19. Verzameld Werk 2, 510, quoted in Muis, *Openbaring*, 359, n.14. The difference in formulation is a good illustration of how Miskotte "appropriated" Barth. He was committed to a theology that is biblically informed. In theory, Barth and Miskotte shared this commitment. A full-scale comparison between Barth and Miskotte is obviously quite beyond the scope of the present work. Surely, Jan Muis has put all Barth and Miskotte scholars in his debt by his thorough analysis.
20. Quoted from Karl Barth, *Church Dogmatics*, I.2; Doctrine of the Word of God, 299f. (Edinburgh: T. & T. Clark, 1988 reprint), quoted in *When the Gods are Silent*, 66.
21. "Die Erlaubnis zu Schriftgemässem Denken," in K. H. Miskotte, *Geloof en Kennis: Theologische Voordrachten* [Faith and Knowledge: Theological Lectures], 163 (Haarlem: Uitgeversmaatschappij Holland, 1966).
22. Muis, *Openbaring*, 358, 359.
23. "Barth practices reflection . . . in which a subject is 'followed,' so that a continuing, if not logical or causal, train of thought emerges. With Miskotte we find less progress from one point to another. He tries to see different phenomena or a number of moments of a phenomenon beside each other." (Ibid., 360, 361).
24. Undoubtedly, Miskotte was quite aware of the scholarship of his landsman, G. Van der Leeuw, author of *Religion in Essence and Manifestation: A Study in Phenomenology*, I, II (New York: Harper & Row, 1963). In chap. 110 of his work, Van der Leeuw offers a concise history of phenomenological research. He begins with the age of Enlightenment, when a Göttingen professor named Meiners wished

to discover what is essential in religion, not stopping at the usual frontier between pagan and Christian; he was not only interested in unique features, but even more in what various religions had in common. During the Romantic era, religious manifestations were regarded as symbols of a primordial revelation. The names of Herder and Schleiermacher were the most important here. Van der Leeuw reserves highest praise for P. D. Chantepie de la Saussaye, and his *Lehrbuch* (1887); his concern was to "comprehend the objective appearances of religion in the light of subjective processes, and accordingly assigned a wide scope to psychology." (Van der Leeuw, *Religion,* II, 694) After that, phenomenology began to dominate the history of religions field. Van der Leeuw mentions W. Wundt, L. Lévy-Bruhl, F. Heiler, Rudolf Otto, and more recently W. Wach, and Van der Leeuw himself (witness the subtitle of his work!) In sum, phenomenology became a dynamic path to the study of the history of religions. Van der Leeuw published his work (in German) in 1933, in the decade when Miskotte did some of his most important writing.

25. *Openbaring,* 361.

26. In *When the Gods are Silent,* for example, he does not only describe the views of other philosophers and his own response as a critical thinker to them, but also moves repeatedly in the area of feeling and experience, as in a statement like the following: "What we are experiencing today can be called an 'eclipse of God' also in the sense that God has been 'stolen,' 'embezzled' from us, not only (or at least not conclusively) through thought but also through the totality of our experience. . . ." (in his discussion of "Eclipse of God," 49).

27. See Muis, *Openbaring,* 361. Various additional differences between Barth and Miskotte are discussed in detail by Muis. Since an English translation of this important work may never see the light of day, his summarizing comments on the subject are quoted here: "In Barth's theology of revelation the hermeneutical problem is taken seriously, but the philosophical solutions of that problem are relativized. His theological determination of the place of human existence is unsurpassable because it takes seriously the confession of the Scriptures as Word of God. Barth's hermeneutic is relevant in five aspects:

1. The biblical writers address us by witnessing what we have not experienced but which is nevertheless determinative for everything we do experience: the life history of the man Jesus, God's special revelation which is generally valid.
2. That revelation is "non-historical" does not mean that it takes place outside of history, but in history as "more-than-history": an act of God.
3. The words of Scripture are only revelatory insofar as they speak to us through and about Christ; they cannot be fully understood therefore without faith and prayer.
4. The orientation on Christ relieves the understanding of the duty to clarify all aspects of the text simultaneously and makes the person who understands flexible and relaxed.
5. The best understanding of Scripture is the retelling in which God's history with man playfully lays hold on us.

By distinguishing revelation and experience, Barth wishes to make room for our experiences, but the manner by which he does so causes many to experience a vacuum. Miskotte fills this vacuum: [by claiming that] believing is living and experiencing [(be)leven]. By bringing into relationship with God life experiences which do not deny the covenant, he makes clear concretely that we do not need to reason away our experience in order to be able to believe. Thought is not better per se, feeling does not need to be mistrusted. We may permit ourselves to be moved along and overpowered. True faith longs for groundless and super-rational delight. This world is not a house of ghosts. We live in God's world.

With Miskotte's hermeneutical processing of the experience and language of the Old Testament, the proclamation of Christ is presupposed. When the apostolic creed functions no longer in the church, the authority [overwicht] of Christ's presence and the serving, referential character of biblical language threatens to be neglected. If the language of Scripture is related to our experience outside of Christ, a structurally different theology emerges." (*Openbaring,* 505)

28. Among the volumes of his published sermons are: *Geloof bij de gratie Gods* [Faith by the Grace of God] (Amsterdam: Uitgeversmaatschappij Holland , 1930); *De vreemde vrijspraak* [The Strange Acquittal] (Amsterdam: Uitgeversmaatschappij Holland, 1938); *Uitkomst: Toespraken voor jongeren van elken leeftijd* [A Way Out: Addresses for Youth of All Ages] (Amsterdam: Uitgeversmaatschappij Holland, 1948); *Gods vijanden vergaan: Preek 9 May 1945* [God's Enemies Perish: Sermon, May 9, 1945] (Amsterdam: Ten Have, 1945); *Feest in de voorhof: Sermoenen voor randbewoners* [Feast in the Forecourt: Sermons for People on the Fringe] (Amsterdam: Uitgeversmaatschappij Holland, 1951); *Miskende Majesteit* [Misunderstood Majesty] (Nijkerk: G. F. Callenbach, 1969); *Gevulde stilte* [Filled Silence] (Kampen: J. H. Kok, 1974); *Geschonken eindigheid* [Finiteness Granted] (Kampen: J. H. Kok, 1978). A number of additional titles were published in Amsterdam by Uitgeversmaatschappij Holland.

29. See note 25, chap. 1 and n. 4, chap. 2.

30. See n.33, chap. 1.

31. Muis, *Openbaring,* 362. In his Foreword, Miskotte says that Part II, "Witness and Interpretation," "deals with the meaning of the Old Testament for our time." (*When the Gods are Silent,* xvii)

Chapter 3. Church and Synagogue

1. Undoubtedly, Miskotte has contributed significantly to the increased sensitivity toward Jews and Judaism in the Netherlands since World War II. In this respect also, he is one of the founding fathers of the Amsterdam School (biblical/theological stance of the University of Amsterdam; see *De Bijbel maakt school; een Amsterdamse weg in de exegese* [The Bible goes Academic: An Amsterdam Path in Exegesis], eds., K. Deurloo, R. Zuurmond (Baarn: Ten Have, 1984). Prof. Doberstein (late Professor, Lutheran Theological Seminary, Philadelphia), translator of *When the Gods are Silent,* claims that the value of that book is that it opens up the possibility of a dialogue with Judaism (ix).

2. He commented somewhere that in answer to "the word" one could respond in one of three ways: Christian, Jew, or pagan. See de Kruijf, *Heiden, Jood en Christen,* 15, n. 52.

3. See n. 26, chap. 1.

4. With his customary frankness, he opens his dissertation as follows: "Busy with a study concerning the doctrine of sanctification in the preaching of Hermann Friedrich Kohlbrügge, the writer of this study, turned into a side-path, forced by the word-analysis of K., by concepts suggested by the Hebrew, and discovered there the possibility, to view the Old Testament as a unique spiritual world, while Judaism did not present itself at all as a '*Vorstufe*' of Christendom, but as a religion sui generis, which as such would not need fulfillment or supplement." (*Wezen der Joodse Religie,* 1)

5. Ibid. P. T. Tomson writes: "As is well known, Karl Barth is the first who incorporated Israel as a theme in dogmatics. But the Jews remain . . . silent figures with him. With Miskotte, articulated Jewish faith is allowed to speak, and it finds with him an open ear and an attentive heart." ("K. H. Miskotte und das heutige jüdisch-christliche Gespräch." *Nederlands Theologisch Tijdschrift* 44, 15–34).

6. Quoting Wilhelm Vischer, "Das Alte Testament und die Geschichte," *Zwischen den Zeiten* (1921), 41, *Wezen der Joodse Religie*, 2. See also Section 2 of *Die Hebräische Bibel und ihre zweifache Nachgeschichte: Festschrift für Rolf Rendtorff zum 65 Geburtstag*, eds., Erhard Blum et al. (Neukirchen-Vluyn: Neukirchener Verlag, 1990), which contains a number of relevant articles, among them: Paul M. Van Buren, "On Reading Someone Else's Mail," 607–617.

7. This is how the present writer would characterize the mentality of most Christian churches in our time, beginning with the Roman Catholic Church which, until quite recently, would not establish a constructive relationship with the state of Israel, as well as the Protestant traditions, which, in spite of some theologians who speak a different language, often teach that the church has replaced Israel as the chosen people, etc. An additional factor is the putative anti-Semitism of a pioneer of the historical-critical method of biblical scholarship, Julius Wellhausen (1844–1918). See Jon D. Levenson, *The Hebrew Bible, the Old Testament and Historical Criticism: Jews and Christians in Biblical Studies* (Louisville: Westminster/Knox, 1993), 10–15.

8. Readings in European Jewish history should be a required subject for Christian clergy. As highlights of the gruesome manner in which Jews have been treated by Christians through the centuries may be cited the expulsions of Jews from Spain and Portugal (1492) and the attempted extermination of all Jews by Hitler's men (commonly referred to as the Holocaust). A good introduction is Max L. Margolis and Alexander Marx, *A History of the Jewish People* (New York: Atheneum, 1969).

9. For convenience's sake the label "Old Testament" is generally used in this study.

10. Muis, *Openbaring*, 355.

11. Most emphatically, of course, in *Wezen der Joodse Religie* and to a much lesser degree in *When the Gods are Silent.*

12. In *When the Gods are Silent,* since that is essentially a book to let the Old Testament speak to the "fourth man," the modern pagan, but also *Edda en Thora* which addresses modern German paganism vis-à-vis the Bible. His dissertation, *Wezen der Joodse Religie,* was a thorough work meriting a German translation, but since the time was not propitious, it never saw a German edition. Since its publication is limited to its original Dutch (it has already been reprinted in Verzameld Werk 6) its influence has been strictly limited. When it was published, Hitler's band was already very active in Germany and the following year (1933) he became Reich Chancellor.

13. Touw, "*Prof. dr. K. H. Miskotte,*" 27.

14. Miskotte claims that correlation plays an important role in Cohen, but always purely methodological, not as a fundamental concept: generative, a concept dealing with origin, excluding all ontology. He further comments that correlation serves the logical justification of man. "God-for-us" is our guarantee that no guilt or sorrow can remove us from our eternal relationship (*Wezen der Joodse Religie,* 203).

15. In the words of Miskotte: Moral humanity in the historical future is the Messiah. God is the idea of Messianism; Messianism is the realization of God (*Wezen der Joodse Religie,* 205).

16. Ibid., 175.

17. Ibid., 212.

18. Being and becoming are connected to one another insofar as one concept logically requires the other." *Encyclopaedia Judaica* 5 (New York: Macmillan, 1971), 675.

19. *Wezen der Joodse Religie,* 211.

20. Ibid., 458.

21. Ibid., 462. "The Platonic and the prophetic line run together part of the time" (Ibid., 209).

22. Ibid., 483.

23. Ibid.

24. Miskotte develops this idea in his inaugural address at Leiden University ("De practische zin van de eenvoud Gods [The practical sense of the simplicity of God]" in *Geloof en kennis,* 7–28.

25. *Wezen der Joodse Religie,* 496–497.

26. Ibid., 497–498. Here Miskotte is a true Barthian, with a God who is the *ganz Andere.*

27. M. Buber, *I and Thou,* translated by Ronald Gregory Smith (Edinburgh: T. & T. Clark, 1937). This little book, first published in 1923, rendered in English in 1937 and reprinted many times since, has deservedly exercised enormous influence not only among Jews and Christians, but in the entire Western world. It is unquestionably one of the monuments of theological writing of the 20th century. Because the study of Judaism loomed so prominently on Miskotte's intellectual horizon, the subject receives additional attention in some other works of his.

28. "The Question of Judaism," in *When the Gods are Silent,* 309–318. He also wrote an article on the subject, "Het Jodendom als vraag aan de kerk [Judaism Questioning the Church]" in Miskotte, *Grensgebied,* 114–123; reprinted in his *Om de waarheid te zeggen,* 185–193. Perhaps most significant of all (for our purposes) are his comments on two articles of a proposed confession of the Dutch Reformed Church in Dr. K. H. Miskotte, *De kern van de zaak: Toelichting bij een proeve van hernieuwd belijden* [The Essence of the Matter: Commentary on a Proof of Renewed Confessing] (Nijkerk: G. F. Callenbach, 1950), 42–53, 242–253. They are briefly discussed below. The article on Israel's election is printed in this book as Appendix C.

29. Franz Rosenzweig, *Der Stern der Erlösung,* III, 37 in *When the Gods are Silent,* 310. The English rendering is a paraphrase of W. W. Hallo's translation, *The Star of Redemption* (New York: Holt, Rinehart and Winston, 1970), 288.

30. The commonly indicated meanings are "change of mind, remorse," but also "repentance, turning about, conversion." Walter Bauer et al., *A Greek-English Lexicon of the New Testament and Other Early Christian Literature,* second edition (Chicago/London: University of Chicago Press 1979), 512b. "The usual meaning is 'change of mind' or 'conversion' with the full Old Testament nuance. This nuance is important, for it makes a big difference whether the call of Jesus to repent is a call to total conversion or simply a call to sorrow for sin, a change of mind, or acts of restitution." Gerhard Kittel et al., *Theological Dictionary of the New Testament: One volume edition* (Grand Rapids, Mich.: Eerdmans, 1985), 642.

31. *When the Gods are Silent,* 310.

32. See *Three Jewish Philosophers: Philo, Saadya Gaon, Jehuda Halevi,* eds., H. Lewy, et al. (New York: Meridian, 1960).

33. Quoted in *When the Gods are Silent*, 312. Judaism has recognized the religious contributions of Christianity. Leo Trepp writes: "This pluralistic outlook springs from Jewish doctrine and conviction that the road to salvation does not lead

exclusively through its own or any individual faith. 'The righteous of all the world's nations have a share in the world to come' is Jewish teaching." He further points to the Noahide laws which lead to salvation for all who abide by them. *Judaism: Development and Life* (Belmont, Calif.: Dickenson, 1966), 94.

34. After World War II and the Holocaust, in Europe at any rate, such optimism might seem warranted, if only as a reaction. However, fifty years later we are still struggling with anti-Semitism and racism in the West, though the picture is hardly monolithic. In the United States there may not be much overt anti-Semitism, but benign anti-Semitism is widespread, even in the churches.

35. Miskotte mentions Leo Baeck, *Das Evangelium als Urkunde der jüdischen Glaubensgeschichte* (1938); Joseph Klausner, *Jesus of Nazareth* (New York: Macmillan, 1953); *Klausner, From Jesus to Paul* (New York: Macmillan, 1943); S. Sandmel, *The Genius of Paul: A Study in History* (New York: Farrar, 1958); Sandmel, *A Jewish Understanding of the New Testament* (New York: Hebrew Union College Press, 1956); Joseph Jacobs, *Jesus as Others Saw Him: A Retrospect A.D. 54;* Sholem Asch, *The Nazarene* (1939); Max Brod, *Der Meister;* and Franz Werfer, *Paulus unter den Juden* (See *When the Gods are Silent,* 313).

36. When the Gods are Silent, 314.

37. Ibid., 315.

38. Franz Rosenzweig, *Briefe* (1935), 670–671, quoted in *When the Gods are Silent,* 315.

39. Ibid., 316.

40. Commenting on John 19:26,27, an older writer states: "What was valuable and permanent in Judaism has now passed over to Christianity: the 'mother of Jesus' now dwells in the house of His disciple." R. H. Strachan, *The Fourth Gospel: Its Significance and Environment* (London: SCM, 1955), 319.

41. Neither Luther nor Calvin are satisfactory guides on this subject. Both write as we might expect them to. H. A. Oberman in his informative *The Roots of Anti-Semitism in the Age of Renaissance and Reformation* has put Luther's anti-Semitism in a broad historical context, comparing it, for example, to the similar attitudes of Reuchlin, Erasmus, and Eck. Apparently, until 1523 Luther actively lobbied for the elimination of obstacles to conversion. When his best attempts failed, he lapsed into the familiar anti-Jewish rhetoric to the end of his life. The list of the "condemned" usually included: Jews (they come first!), heretics, heathen, sinners, Turks, hypocrites. (Philadelphia: Fortress, 1984, passim.) Luther incorporates his understanding of Paul into his commentary and writes very critically about Jews: "The Jews arrogantly assumed that they were God's people, simply because the heathen were not His people . . . the Jews and the heretics venerate God according to their own mind, and in their stupid zeal and their eccentric piety they are worse than the ungodly." *Commentary on Romans,* trans. J. Theodore Mueller. (Grand Rapids, Mich.: Kregel, 1993), 156f. Calvin, emphasizing election, makes it a very personal affair. It seems that he cannot treat "Israel" as a people. " . . . salvation is freely offered to *some* while *others* are barred from access to it . . . our salvation flows from the wellspring of God's free mercy until we come to know his eternal election, which illumines God's grace by this contrast: that he does not indiscriminately adopt all into the hope of salvation but gives to *some* what he denies to *others.*" *Institutes of the Christian Religion,* III. Italics added. Ed. John T. McNeill, trans. F. L. Battles. (Philadelphia: Westminster, 1960), 21.1. Clearly, Miskotte does not follow either, but charts his own path, based on his reading of the Bible.

42. Paul's argument is to undercut boasting by both Gentiles and Jews, to affirm the righteousness of God. " . . . it is from heir incorporation into the stock of Israel

that Gentile Christians derive their spiritual blessings." C. E. B. Cranfield, *Romans. A Shorter Commentary* (Grand Rapids, Mich.: Eerdmans, 1985), 279.

43. *When the Gods are Silent,* 317.

44. *Kern van de zaak.* See n.28, above.

45. "[Miskotte] is quite capable of a style sometimes so obscure as to be Stygian. Throughout it is dense, compact, and elliptical, full of qualifying phrases, alliterations, and many plays on words." John W. Doberstein, trans. *When the Gods are Silent,* xv.

46. See Appendix C for a translation of this article.

47. New in the sense that "Israel" was not usually treated as a confessional *topos.*

48. *Kern van de zaak,* 42.

49. Ibid., 43.

50. Ibid., 44.

51. This is a familiar motif in Dutch (Reformed) Christianity, since it was often appended to the *Votum* (opening sentence): "Our help is in the name of the Lord, who made heaven and earth, *who is faithful forever and does not abandon the work of his hands.*"

52. A typical Barthian motif! *Church Dogmatics,* II.2, chap. 7, §33: The Election of Jesus Christ. (Edinburg: T. & T. Clark, 1957)

53. *Kern van de zaak,* 45.

54. The view that divine predestination did not precede creation, but that it was after the fall (Genesis 3) that God decreed his election of humans to salvation.

55. *Kern van de zaak,* 45. This comment reads like his response to the (Jewish) doctrine of correlation.

56. Ibid., 46. The dynamic relationship between the particular and the general needs to be maintained. This is Miskotte's way of indicating the way of experience and knowledge in divine revelation. Van der Star writes: "This irreversible relationship is as it were a curve which may never be fixed in a single point, but is only to be understood in its movement and tendency. . . . The one implies the other." H. C. van der Star, "Zien op het gehoor af: Enkele structurele aspecten van Miskottes theologische cultuuranalyse [Seeing what we Hear: Some Structural Aspects of Miskotte's Theological Analysis of Culture]" in *Horen en Zien: Opstellen over de theologie van K. H. Miskotte;* [Hearing and Seeing: Essays on the Theology of K. H. Miskotte]. Eds. H. W. de Knijff and G. W. Neven (Kampen: J. H. Kok, 1991), 97f. The relationship may not be strictly reversible, but, as Eric Crump of Gettysburg Lutheran Seminary suggests, be more like a back and forth movement.

57. Phil. 3:15, after extended comments on appropriate Christian behavior, labels those who follow these words τελειοι: full-grown, mature, complete, having reached their utmost development. Cf. also Eph. 4:13, Heb. 5:14. The Old Testament uses the concept of holiness to describe the divinely demanded quality of life: wihyîtem lî qĕdōšîm kî qādôš ›anî yhwh wā›abdīl ’etkem min-hā‘ammîm lihyôt lî [You shall be holy to me, for I YHWH am holy, and I have separated (this verb is often used in the Genesis 1 creation account) you from the other peoples to be mine], Lev. 20:26. Here, election and holiness are linked, as Miskotte emphasizes.

58. *Kern van de zaak,* 47–48 (see n.53).

59. Ibid., 50. This critique is quoted here in full to counteract the notion that Miskotte is not sufficiently critical of Judaism, that he has gone too far in his appreciation of that faith.

60. Ibid., 51.

61. Ibid., 243.

62. For many, he goes too far in one direction. After all, he has generally been quite critical both of Judaism and Christianity. It might have been better to say that *both* are in need of conversion, but which religion enjoys hearing that? All of this goes to show how incredibly difficult it is to engage in fruitful religious dialogue.

63. Ibid., 244. He is clearly comparing the two on the basis of biological/ sociological cohesiveness (bonding), in which Judaism has an obvious advantage, compared to the church as a "melting pot."

64. Ibid., 246. Bonhoeffer had little use for liturgical revival, as if that would counteract secularization: "Only he who cries out for the Jews, dare also sing in Gregorian." Quoted in *When the Gods are Silent,* 82. The situation is no better on the American scene, where prayers for the Jews (if they are said at all!) may more often than not relate to their hoped for conversion! K. A. D. Smelik has written: "Only after one has truly learned to know Judaism, one may venture to reflect dogmatically on the relationship between church and synagogue," *Anti-Judaïsme en kerk* [Anti Judaism and Church] [Baarn: Ten Have, 1993)] , 130, quoted in *Kornelis Heiko Miskotte (1894–1976): Brug tussen cultuur & theologie* [Kornelis Heiko Miskotte (1894–1976): Bridge between Culture and Theology], eds. A. C. den Besten et al. (Kampen: J. H. Kok, 1995), 74.

65. "Irrevocable" (αμεταμελητα) is a legal term, meaning "not to be repeated or regretted."

66. *Kern van de zaak,* 247.

67. Ibid., 248.

68. As discussed above, this statement is locally conditioned. There is no question that Protestant sentiment, at any rate in favor of Israel, is much stronger in parts of Europe than in America. Many Dutch churches took special offerings for Israel during the Six Day War of June, 1967.

69. The word "reformed" is rendered in two ways in Dutch. The original Calvinist church was called *Gereformeerd* which is akin to French *réformé.* When William I, Holland's first king, in the early 19th century (after the Napoleonic era), decided he wanted an established (state) church, the church was renamed Dutch Reformed: *Nederlands Hervormde Kerk* (the Germanic prefix *her–* was used to replace the French *re–*; the meaning is the same). Subsequent church-splits revived the label *Gereformeerd,* much to the chagrin of Miskotte, who thought that *Gereformeerd,* being the original name of the Dutch church, should be honored again by the historic Dutch Reformed Church.

70. Since almost half a century ago when this was written, it sounds almost prophetic, at least as far as the United States is concerned.

71. Robert H. Gundry, *Matthew: A Commentary on His Literary and Theological Art.* (Grand Rapids, Mich.: Eerdmans, 1982), 565.

72. "Martin Buber" in Dr K. H. Miskotte, *In de Waagschaal: Gekozen en ingeleid door W. Barnard en Dr. J. J. Buskes* [In the Balance: Selected and Introduced by W. Barnard and Dr. J. J. Buskes] (Amsterdam: Uitgeversmaatschappij Holland, 1960), 138.

73. Ibid., 139.

74. See the discussion on "correlation," chap. 3, section 3.

75. Liturgical renewal, which now routinely prescribes a reading from the Old Testament for every Sunday (except during the Easter season) does not mean that worshippers are well versed or well taught in the story of ancient Israel. Superficial preaching by pastors who are themselves insufficiently trained in the Old Testament,

Miskotte might say, can only produce ill-fed Christians—in his terminology, representatives of the "third man . . . in the pipeline to nihilism."

Chapter 4. Religion, Paganism, and Nihilism

1. As readers have seen correctly, this book is a pastoral guide "for the perplexed, an exposition of how the Old Testament speaks to the situation of 'the fourth man.'" (*When the Gods are Silent,* x)

2. Quoted in *When the Gods are Silent,* 244, from Martin Buber and Franz Rosenzweig, *Die Schrift und ihre Verdeutschung* (Berlin: Schocken, 1936), 45. This important work is now available in English translation: *Scripture and Translation,* trans. Lawrence Rosenwald with Everett Fox (Bloomington/Indianapolis: Indiana University Press, 1994).

3. *Church Dogmatics* I.1, (Edinburgh: T. & T. Clark, 1936), sec. 5.2, 132, 133.

4. Ibid., I.2, sec. 17.2, 299, 300.

5. According to Miskotte, Bonhoeffer asked the question of the continued relevance of the outward aspects of faith, such as church, preaching, liturgy in a religionless world (*When the Gods are Silent,* 80).

6. Ibid., 11.

7. Ibid., 66.

8. Ibid., 38f.

9. Ibid., 62. In each of these cases, a static word has replaced a dynamic, personal, and relational label.

10. Ibid., 125. This is based on Miskotte's asertion that the name of YHWH is primary, not one name among others (123).

11. *Edda en Thora,* 16. Miskotte sporadically refers to Islam and Buddhism (as in *When the Gods are Silent*) but the index fails to list Hinduism, Confucianism, or Taoism.

12. *Openbaring*, 424.

13. *When the Gods are Silent,* 187.

14. The differences in historical orientation between *Edda en Thora* (published 1939) and *When the Gods are Silent* (1956) should be noted. Miskotte interpreted the events of the thirties as a revival of paganism, which was never conquered by Christianity. In his (specific) study of Old Norse paganism (Edda) he generalized to make it characteristic of all paganism. See G. G. de Kruijf, "Miskottes fenomenologische benadering van de cultuur [Miskotte's Phenomenological Approach to Culture]" in *Horen en zien,* 20, 21. H. J. Heering has criticized Miskotte for relating a way of thought to a people in *Edda en Thora* (Muis, *Openbaring,* 422, n.134). However, this is what Miskotte saw and experienced in Europe of the mid-thirties. The scars caused by the Nazis have not yet healed in Europe. Neither have the Germans always been anxious to face up to their relatively recent past! The problem appears even more difficult in Japan.

15. *Edda en Thora,* 29.

16. Ibid., 28.

17. Muis, *Openbaring,* 423, where he refers to *When the Gods are Silent,* the section "The Twofold Action of the Scriptures," 59. There is a kind of "interface" in the church where there are representatives of "the third man," who have difficulty distinguishing God from the gods and the godhead. In that milieu, Miskotte seeks to "unmask religion." One of the stumbling blocks is supposed familiarity with the

Scriptures, which has led people astray. See also chap. 4, "Religion," for his comments on the "continuum."

18. J. Janeff, *Dämonie des Jahrhunderts* (1939), 349, quoted in *Edda en Thora,* 24, and in *When the Gods are Silent,* 8.

19. *When the Gods are Silent,* 8.

20. Ibid., 224. That was written in the mid-fifties; one wonders what he would say today with the sprouting of Neo-Nazi movements in Germany, Italy, the United States and elsewhere.

21. *When the Gods are Silent,* 226.

22. Ibid., 7.

23. De Kruijf, summarizing, writes that paganism shuns common sense and sharp distinctions; experienced reality is everything; thus, God and the world are mixed. The world is not created, for that would imply boundaries which are not recognized. Chaos rules, there is no history, the cosmos is constantly becoming and in motion, but without a goal or purpose. *Miskottes fenomenologische benadering,* 21.

24. God is not "ens realissimum" or "summum bonum." (Muis, *Openbaring,* 423, n.140)

25. *When the Gods are Silent,* 217, 218.

26. Ibid., 306.

27. Ibid., 309, and chap. 3.

28. *When the Gods are Silent,* 432.

29. *Horen en zien,* 133–150.

30. Ibid., 133.

31. Even the concept of "truth," an offshoot of metaphysics, is rejected by Nietzsche. Using a term or a label is no guarantee that something exists. Miskotte followed Nietzsche's radical critique: he remained suspicious of traditional statements about God. See *Miskotte over God,* 135.

32. *When the Gods are Silent,* 15, 16.

33. Ibid., 17.

34. Ibid., 20, 22.

35. *Miskotte over God,* 134. Neven also cites Francis Fukuyama who, in a controversial article entitled "Het einde van de geschiedenis [The End of History]" in *De groene Amsterdammer* 113 (1989) 51,52 avers that many of life's abstract goals, capacity for imagination and idealism will be replaced by economic calculation, the endless solving of technical problems, and the satisfaction of the "refined needs" of the consumer. "In the post-historic period neither art nor philosophy will be mentioned; only the perpetual care of the museum of history will remain."

36. Miskotte, *Bijbels ABC,* 12.

37. Neven, "Miskotte over God," 138.

38. To mention a single example: discussing themes common to both Testaments which are more fully treated in the Old Testament, he writes that in such cases we need to go back to the Old Testament, "which as it gives its independent witness, demands that it be allowed to speak 'for itself.'" *When the Gods are Silent,* 262.

39. Neven cites F. Rosenzweig, *Der Stern der Erlösung,* 116–120 in "Miskotte over God," 140.

40. Miskotte referred more than once to the "errors" of his church, particularly its organization (not its faith, which, he said, was the faith of the fathers). He writes: "I personally (with many others) consider that the time has come for far-reaching changes in this organization [of the Dutch Reformed Church], but not without gratefully recognizing the good service which this old [organization] of

1816 has rendered to all of our people . . . the intended change can never be 'back to 1618,' [as the seceded groups insisted] but always 'forward! on to a deeper and broader relationship to the needs of our time and to the future of the Lord.'" . . . *als een die dient*, 261.

41. *When the Gods are Silent*, 98.

Chapter 5. The Old Testament

1. *When the Gods are Silent*, xi.
2. *Openbaring*, 361.
3. *When the Gods are Silent*, 170.
4. Ibid., 173.
5. John Calvin was also concerned with laying the two testaments side by side. See his *Institutes*, II, xi.
6. There is still a debate going on whether the label Tenak or Tanakh for the Hebrew Bible (Old Testament) is also appropriate for Christians to use. Whatever label is preferred, the Jewish order of books is simpler and more sensible than the customary "Christian" order which represents an unfortunate attempt at listing the books in some sort of historical order (such as placing Ruth after Judges and the Writings [Hagiographa] before the Latter Prophets). Miskotte has an excellent discussion on the Torah (Pentateuch) in *When the Gods are Silent* (228–246) and also discusses Prophetism (288–295). It is reported that the Jewish order of books is being restored in French Bibles.
7. *When the Gods are Silent*, 95.
8. Ibid., 308.
9. Ibid., 333.
10. Ibid., 334. Their attitude toward life and politics was inspired by the prophetism of the Old Testament; it led to high ethical standards with "respect for the potentialities of the ordinary man."
11. Ibid., 61. "Ungenuine nihilism" is defined by Miskotte as "rebelling conformism," the situation of the fourth man who is confused.
12. Ibid., 62.
13. See chap. 6, "Acts of God."
14. *When the Gods are Silent*, 309.
15. Ibid., 241.
16. To mention a single example, he claims that the Talmud represents two opposing notions, namely to isolate the transcendent God deistically, and to bring the transcendent God in polar community with man (*Wezen der Joodse Religie*, 554). In modern Israel, Miskotte says, selections from all three parts of the Tanak are broadcast daily, which leads him to express the fear "that a new self-satisfied religion is coming into being and manifesting itself more and more confidently." (*When the Gods are Silent*, 57, 58)
17. *Bijbels ABC*, 13.
18. Muis, *Openbaring*, 401.
19. See R. Oost, *Omstreden bijbeluitleg: Aspecten en achtergronden van de hermeneutische discussie rondom de exegese van het Oude Testament in Nederland* [Controversial Biblical Exegesis: Aspects and Background of the Hermeneutical Discussion concerning the Exegesis of the Old Testament in The Netherlands]. Dissertation, Groningen, 1986 (Kampen: J. H. Kok, 1986), 21–23. Uwe Bauer, כל הדברים האלה All diese Worte: Impulse zur Schiftauslegung aus Amster-

dam. Expliziert an der Schilfmeererzählung in Exodus 13,17–14,31, 56–70. Dissertation, Amsterdam, 1991 (Frankfurt am Main: Lang, 1991) and *Voices from Amsterdam: A Modern Tradition of Reading Biblical Narrative*, ed. by Martin Kessler (Atlanta: Scholars Press, 1994). See "Introduction," ix–xxiii.

20. This translation, begun by Martin Buber and Franz Rosenzweig, was completed by Buber alone because of Rosenzweig's untimely death in 1929. Buber kept making changes in the translation, which has gone through many editions. The current printing is the eighth of the 1958 edition, published by the Deutsche Bibelgesellschaft, Stuttgart (1992), in four paperback volumes: *Die fünf Bücher der Weisung* [Torah], *Bücher der Geschichte* [Former Prophets], *Bücher der Kündung* [Latter Prophets], and *Die Schriftwerke* [Writings].

21. In his Introduction to his dissertation, he explains how he came to his subject: as he was studying sanctification in the preaching of Kohlbrügge, he checked the Hebrew roots to which Kohlbrügge had referred (*Wezen der Joodse Religie,* 1).

22. *Levende Woord,* 83.

23. *When the Gods are Silent,* 152.

24. The esthetic approach, which appreciates "die Schönheit der Bibel" and practices "close reading," has made enormous headway since Miskotte wrote. This is not reducing the biblical writing to "art for art's sake" (if there is such a thing!), but rather insisting that the artful form of the language in which Scripture is clothed is the chosen vehicle of communication. In spite of Nietzsche's derogatory comments to the contrary, the New Testament also has many specimens of highly artistic literature.

25. *When the Gods are Silent,* 160.

26. *Bijbels ABC,* 92 (emphasis added).

27. *Wezen der Joodse Religie,* 520.

28. *When the Gods are Silent,* 159.

29. Rochus Zuurmond, Old Testament Professor at the University of Amsterdam, tells the story of a visit by a group of friends to Frans Breukelman, eminent Amsterdam Old Testament scholar (often regarded as the founding father of the "Amsterdam School"), on his fiftieth birthday. Tom Naastepad, one of the guests, told a story of Breukelman's entry into heaven. St. Peter would immediately ask him to preach, and in heaven that was only done by the best! The only preaching allowed in heaven was from the only Bible that satisfied all exegetical requirements: *an Old Testament, in which all of the New Testament was printed in footnotes.* (R. Zuurmond, "Opnieuw Om het levende Woord: Een woord vooraf [Again: Around the Living Word. A Word of Introduction]" *Om het levende Woord: Bijbelstheologische en dogmatische uitgave van het Delenus-Instituut,* 2.3, emphasis added. (Kampen: J. H. Kok, 1993) This work is not to be confused with a 1948 publication by the same title. See n.41, chap. 1.

30. *Edda en Thora,* 385.

31. German equivalent: Gestalt; Greek μορφη, Latin figura. In this work, the translation of (Dutch) "gestalte" depends on the context.

32. H. Berkhof, "De hermeneutiek van Miskotte en het Oude Testament, I [The hermeneutic of Miskotte and the Old Testament]." *In de Waagschaal* 9 (1980), 141, quoted in Bauer, *All diese Worte,* 61, to whom thanks are due for several references in this section. The background for this affirmation is that for Barth "Word" signifies "self-revelation" whereas Miskotte stresses "address." This also implies that Miskotte puts more emphasis on the role of the Scriptures as "written Word." See his sub-section "The Spoken Word" in *When the Gods are Silent,* 336–340.

33. Muis, *Openbaring,* 379.

34. Barth, *Church Dogmatics*, I.2, 83.

35. *Bijbels ABC*, 42, 43.

36. In the words of Muis: "The unity of Scripture as human word corresponds with the unity of the Word of God and the unity of the Name. As with Miskotte the Word of God and Scripture are closer together in his doctrine of revelation than with Barth, in his epistemology he joins theology to phenomenology." (*Openbaring*, 485).

37. Barth, *Church Dogmatics* I.1, 120.

38. Influenced by Rosenzweig, "life" was an important theological motif for Miskotte, particularly in his Zeitspiegel where he writes that the Name points to life (*When the Gods are Silent*, 73). In the section "The Tree of Life" he quotes a thought from Israel's wisdom literature, to the effect that wisdom brings life (351). Miskotte interprets the Tree of Life as "a quiet presence . . . almost . . . a sacramental sign that confirms . . . that YHWH's purpose for man is altogether good." (353). The life that God intended is to be lived by the Torah (361).

39. Muis, *Openbaring*, 481.

40. Muis, *Openbaring*, 241, who refers to Barth, *Church Dogmatics* I.2, 88–131.

41. Mathias Gutzmann refers to the Dutch theologian A. A. van Ruler, for whom the Old Testament is the real Bible, with the Christian church and the New Testament functioning to explain the Old. The Calvinist tradition of Dutch theology has led Miskotte to be more reticent. (*Die Theologie von Kornelis Heiko Miskotte [1894–1976] in ihrem zeitgeschichtlichen und problemgeschichtlichen Kontext: Schriftliche Hausarbeit im Rahmen der Ersten Staatsprüfung für das Lehramt für die Sekundarstufe* II.) (Paderborn Universität, 1993), 48, n.147.

42. This carries no pejorative connotation whatever for Miskotte. He objects to the idea that the Old Testament should be "lower" than the New Testament. He sees as the benefit of approaching his subject in this manner: to get away from the spell of religion (*When the Gods are Silent*, 173).

43. *Israel: Its Life and Culture*, I, II (London: Oxford University Press, 1926/1940).

44. See n.2, chap. 4.

45. London: 1960.

46. Cardiff: University of Wales Press, 1942.

47. New York: Harper & Row, 1963.

48. *When the Gods are Silent*, 180.

49. Ibid., 191–199. See chap. 5, "The Unity of Scripture," and chap. 6, "Prophecy."

50. See chap. 6.

51. *When the Gods are Silent*, 193.

52. Ibid., 197. G. E. Wright wrote *God Who Acts: Biblical Theology as Recital* (Studies in Biblical Theology, 8; Chicago: Allenson, 1952) four years before Miskotte wrote his *When the Gods are Silent*. See n.61, chap. 6.

53. *When the Gods are Silent*, 198.

54. Ibid., 205.

55. See n.50, above.

56. Quoting "Binnen den Pinkstercirkel [Within the Pentecost Circle]" in *Jeugd en Kampwerk* (N. C. S. V., 1925), *When the Gods are Silent*, 221.

57. Ibid., 222.

58. Ibid., 223.

59. Ibid., 224.

60. Ibid., 264–271.

61. Ibid., 270.

62. Ibid., 271.

63. "If we . . . ignore the Old Testament or merely recite it but do not expound and proclaim it, we shall miss the proper 'point of contact' for the kerygma. That is to say, listening to the Old Testament is the one point of contact upon which the hearing of the New Testament depends; and . . . we must allow it to speak for itself." (*When the Gods are Silent,* 283.)

64. Miskotte calls it "an unpromising undertaking to try to discover or reconstruct a true text . . . the 'true' history behind the text." (When the Gods are Silent, 145) Presently, a great debate is taking place among Old Testament scholars as to which Jeremiah text we ought to use for exegesis. For many scholars the answer is: *the MT [fairly drastically] "improved" by the LXX.* It seems unlikely that Miskotte would have agreed.

65. Miskotte refers to Rosenzweig, *Der Stern der Erlösung,* II, 49ff.

66. Buber, in his *I and Thou,* speaks of the "primary words," I-Thou, signifying relationship and mutuality (Edinburgh: Clark, 1953 reprint, 3–8). In an article on Franz Rosenzweig, Miskotte speaks of language and grammar as a metaphor of life, with special attention to verb and noun ("Over Franz Rosenzweig," in *Geloof en Kennis,* 278).

67. It was also Rosenzweig's. (See n.38 above) He ends his *Stern der Erlösung* with a panegyric on the subject. Miskotte speaks of worship renewing contact with "Life-itself" (*Kern van de Zaak,* 118). While believing in "eternal life," Miskotte's theology was strongly this-worldly. See the section "Out into Life" in *When the Gods are Silent,* 71–73, and Muis, *Openbaring,* 363, 364.

68. As does 1 John 1:1 (prologue) where "the word of life" is stated as the topic of the letter, which is capable of being heard, seen, and touched.

69. *Antwoord uit het onweer,* 311, 312.

70. *When the Gods are Silent,* 146.

71. *Levende Woord,* 38. Emphasis added. Neven claims that Miskotte was influenced by his study of Judaism in the development of his exegetical method. (G. W. Neven, "Miskotte over 'God voor en na zijn dood' [Miskotte about 'God before and after his death']" in *Horen en zien,* 141). Miskotte's exegetical method also seems to tie in well with his penchant for phenomenology.

72. *Levende Woord,* 41.

73. *When the Gods are Silent,* 262. Italics added.

74. *When the Gods are Silent,* 41. When Miskotte wrote this work (1956, the Dutch edition), biblical criticism was almost exclusively in the diachronic mode ([inappropriately] called "literary criticism") though some voices critical of that method were heard in the Netherlands: B. D. Eerdmans of Leiden, in a different vein Juda Palache of Amsterdam, and internationally, Martin Buber and Franz Rosenzweig. Miskotte stressed that the Bible should be studied critically: the best literary criticism available should be consulted.

75. In his writing, Miskotte normally referred to what were considered the best contemporary critical sources of biblical scholarship.

76. *Levende Woord,* 44.

77. *Levende Woord,* 48. At the conclusion of chapter 2 of this book, which deals with the practice of exegesis, Miskotte writes: "The science of exegesis has more or less failed if it has not given us delight and joy, in the midst of the melancholic relativism of the world and of our humanity. Tears often open our eyes and cries open up our ears. But that with our eyes and ears open we might see the King in his beauty—that is the goal [of exegesis]." (170)

78. In *The Word of God and the Word of Man* (New York: Harper, 1957), 28–50.
79. *Bijbels ABC*, 11–18.
80. Ibid., 11.
81. Ibid., 12.
82. Ibid., 13.
83. Ibid., 14, 15.
84. A collection of articles which he contributed to this journal are printed in *In de waagschaal*. See n.73, chap. 3. Also: K. H. Miskotte, *In de Waagschaal: Een keur uit de artikelen van Dr. K. H. Miskotte uit de eerste vijf jaargangen van In de Waagschaal.* [In the Balance: A Selection from the articles by Dr. K. H. Miskotte from the first five volumes of In de Waagschaal]. Verzameld Werk 1 (Kampen: J. H. Kok, 1982).
85. Miskotte, *Zur biblischen Hermeneutik*. This essay is reprinted (in German) in *Geloof en Kennis*, 200–229.
86. *Hermeneutik*, 4.
87. Sendbrief vom Dolmetschen," dated September 8, 1530, quoted in *Hermeneutik*, 5.
88. Quoted, Ibid., 6.
89. Miskotte notes not only the increase in numbers (5, 20, 100) but also the types of work in apparently increasing difficulty: shepherd/farmer, statesman, pastor.
90. *Hermeneutik*, 7. See chapter 6.
91. Ibid., 8.
92. Ibid., 8, 9.

Chapter 6. The Biblical ABCs

1. The difficulty of Miskotte's writing has already been commented on. As in the case of Karl Barth, Miskotte's writing has been thought to have been improved by translation, at which time cooperation between author and translator occasioned helpful clarification. Fr. W. Marquardt writes: "He [Miskotte] was an exceptionally reflective thinker; the main points of his work are not easily systematized." ("'Bijbelse houding' bij Barth en 'bijbelse alefbetisering van de theologie' bij Miskotte," ["Biblical attitude" of Barth and "Biblical Alphabetizing of Theology" with Miskotte] in *Horen en zien*, 33).
2. *When the Gods are Silent*, 51.
3. See n.20, chap. 2.
4. Muis, *Openbaring*, 379.
5. *When the Gods are Silent*, 52.
6. Th. C. Vriezen, *Hoofdlijnen der Theologie van het Oude Testament* (Wageningen: H. Veenman, 1954), 105.
7. *Levende Woord*, 75. Countless times we find the expression: "The word of YHWH came [happened!] to . . ." (היה) or "and YHWH spoke to Moses, saying . . ." Whereas the word moves in the area of Torah (teaching, instruction), it is specific, for communication to persons: to one, or to a whole people, depending on the stated addressee.
8. *Bijbels ABC*, 99.
9. *Levende Woord*, 112.
10. Ibid., 168; Muis, *Openbaring*, 379.
11. *Levende Woord*, 75.

12. *Bijbels ABC,* 97.
13. Ibid., 100, 101.
14. He lives, biblically speaking, lipnê yhwh, *or: coram Deo.*
15. *Bijbels ABC,* 101.
16. Ibid., 102.
17. Buber speaks of the "disintegration" of the Word because religion removed its form (*I and Thou,* 119).
18. Ibid., 103. Though that time seems distant history presently, our world nevertheless has enormous difficulty maintaining the purity of the word because of the declining quality of speech, which in turn relates to progressive decadence and to the propensity that puts much stock in wanting to be entertained, very often in a context where speech is shut out, superfluous, or irrelevant.
19. Muis, *Openbaring,* 489–491.
20. Ibid., 491.
21. Ibid., 494.
22. The verb "happens" was deliberately chosen; the Hebrew is היה as in the common phrase reporting the "reception of revelation" ויהי דבר יהוה.
23. *Bijbels ABC,* 11.
24. Ibid., 32.
25. See chap. 5 (Scripture) and 6 (Acts of God).
26. Bijbels ABC, 33.
27. *When the Gods are Silent,* 119
28. E. Jacob, *Theology of the Old Testament* (New York: Harper, 1958), 82. Miskotte writes that speaking anthropomorphically about God is not to be excused because of the limitation of human understanding, but rather because of the Name, the form [gestalte] that God assumes in his revelation. (*Bijbels ABC,* 40)
29. Jacob, *Theology of the Old Testament,* 83.
30. G. von Rad, *Studies in Deuteronomy,* 38 (Studies in Biblical Theology, 9. Chicago: Regnery, 1953).
31. Jacob, *Theology of the Old Testament,* 85.
32. Muis, *Openbaring,* 366.
33. Miskotte refers to this phrase ten times in *When the Gods are Silent.* He firmly rejects the common rendering (still in the NRSV) "I am who I am" (97). Rather, he takes the "imperfect" verbal form as a future: "I will be as I will be" (290) or "I will be there as I will be there" (297) or "I will be with you as I will be with you" (338).
34. Muis, *Openbaring,* 366.
35. *Gecroonde allemansgading,* 27. The article cited is supposed to have been published ca. 1917, when Miskotte was about 23 years old.
36. *Bijbels ABC,* chap. 3, 32–41.
37. *When the Gods are Silent,* 32.
38. *Edda en Thora,* 13.
39. *Bijbels ABC,* 33.
40. As has often been pointed out, the view of the Hebrew Bible is monolatry, not monotheism.
41. "Indeed, even though there may be so-called gods in heaven or on earth—as in fact there are many gods and many lords—yet for us there is one God, the Father, from whom are all things and for whom we exist, and one Lord, Jesus Christ, through whom are all things and through whom we exist." See K. A. Deurloo, "Monotheïsme is niet bijzonder, [Monotheism is not unique] in *Kornelis Heiko Miskotte (1894–1976),* 157–166.

42. *Bijbels ABC,* 36.
43. Ibid., 34.
44. Ibid., 37. Miskotte's last book(?) is *De Weg van het Gebed* (Den Haag, 1980, sixth printing) = *Der Weg des Gebets* (Munich, 1964) = *The Road of Prayer,* trans. J. W. Doberstein (New York, 1968). Reportedly this has also been translated in Italian.
45. See n.33, chap. 6.
46. *Bijbels ABC,* 43.
47. Ibid.
48. Ibid., 44. Jan Muis discusses this aspect of Miskotte's thought under the heading: "The Scripture as echo of the Name" (*Openbaring,* 413–433). He writes: "That God reveals himself in the one man Jesus, becomes intelligible through anthropomorphic speaking about the Name in the Old Testament. That the Name refers to all does not deny, but presupposes that he is experienced in special encounters by people. Not only the Name, [but] life also demands that we go from the particular to the general, from experience to thought." (432) See also David S. Yeago, "The New Testament and the Nicene Dogma: A Contribution to the Recovery of Theological Exegesis," *Pro Ecclesia* 3 (1994), 152–164.
49. Part II, chap. 3: The Surplus, section on Prophetism (288–295) and chap. 4: Authority and Outgoing of the Word, the first section, Prophecy and History (303–309).
50. Gerhard von Rad, *Theologie des Alten Testaments,* 2,102, quoted in *When the Gods are Silent,* 289.
51. Abraham J. Heschel, *The Prophets* (New York: Harper & Row, 1962), 2.1–11.
52. *When the Gods are Silent,* 290.
53. Ibid., 291, 292.
54. Ibid., 292.
55. Ibid., 293. See chap. 6, Acts of God section.
56. Ibid., 294. The closing words of Buber's *I and Thou* might be read in this context.
57. Ibid.
58. Quoted from G. van der Leeuw, *De Bijbel als boek,* 6 in *When the Gods are Silent,* 303.
59. He repeatedly makes this point in *When the Gods are Silent* (243, 262, 283, 421, 461, 468).
60. *Bijbels ABC,* 84.
61. Wright, *God Who Acts,* 84. It seems unlikely that Wright was familiar with Miskotte's work, from which he might have profited.
62. *Bijbels ABC,* 90.
63. Ibid., 91.
64. Ibid., 55.
65. Ibid.
66. See chap. 5., Old Testament Interpretations section.
67. *Bijbels ABC,* 56, 57.
68. Ibid., 57.
69. Ibid., 60.
70. Ibid., 61. Emphasis added.
71. The LXX normally renders tôrāh as νομος—which is usually translated as "law or rule governing one's actions, principle, norm."
72. *When the Gods are Silent,* 228, 229.

73. *Bijbels ABC*, 19.
74. *When the Gods are Silent*, 230.
75. *Bijbels ABC*, 20.
76. Miskotte speaks of *kijken* [to look], *zien* [to see], and *horen* [to hear]. On the exegetical plane, these are analogous to 1. literary-historical criticism, 2. phenomenology, and 3. theological exegesis. (*Levende Woord*, 38) See also chap. 5, "Exegesis."
77. *When the Gods are Silent*, 230.
78. Ibid., 231.
79. Ibid.
80. *Bijbels ABC*, 22.
81. *Gecroonde Allemansgading*, 253–268.
82. *Bijbels ABC*, 23.
83. Ibid. Miskotte frequently attacks bourgeois ways of thinking, which he considers a substantial obstacle to the reception of the Word.
84. Ibid., 24.
85. Ibid., 25.
86. *When the Gods are Silent*, 106.
87. *Bijbels ABC*, 25. In the Dutch Reformed tradition, confirmation is traditionally called "confession of faith" or "acceptance" or "reception" [aanneming].
88. Ibid., 26.
89. Ibid., 27.
90. Ibid., 27, 28.
91. This is a typically Dutch way of describing the unchurched multitude. In our country, the illusion of church membership and of "being a Christian" blinds many to the fact that countless of our contemporaries are, if not to be labeled representatives of the "fourth man" certainly qualify as representatives of the "third man."
92. In an article "Balans van Nederland [Balance of the Netherlands]," 1945. Quoted, *Bijbels ABC*, 30.
93. Ibid.
94. Ibid., 31.
95. There are a few exceptions, Torah and Tanak being the main examples.
96. From the root hlk (to walk), hălākāh constitutes the body of legal decisions directing the Jews' "walk" in life.
97. Meaning: "way, path"; it occurs 710 times in the Hebrew Bible.
98. *Bijbels ABC*, 108.
99. See " . . . *als een die dient*," 254 and passim. The phrase was likely suggested by the rhymed text of Psalm 25, stanza 7 (1773 version):

Gods verborgen omgang vinden,
zielen, waar zijn vrees in woont;
't heilgeheim wordt aan zijn vrinden,
naar zijn vreêverbond getoond . . .

Translation (in the prose mode): "God's hidden 'contact' finds souls, in which his fear dwells; the salvific secret is shown to his friends, according to his covenant of peace." Clearly, this is paraphrastic, as are all the Dutch rhymed psalms. Naturally, such a concept is unintelligible to those who keep talking as if God were the "perpetually available," as if he were a kind of deus ex machina, responding to our beck and call. In *When the Gods are Silent*, Miskotte wrote that an "eclipse of God" was experienced in these times (he wrote in 1956, but he might have said the same about 1941(!) when he wrote *Bijbels ABC*).

100. *Bijbels ABC*, 109.

101. *Ibid.*, 111.

102. Buber renders "Freiheit."

103. Scholars who are considered representative of "the Amsterdam School" have acknowledged their indebtedness to Miskotte, as well as to Martin Buber and Franz Rosenzweig. Frans Breukelman is usually considered to be the closest link between Miskotte and the Amsterdam School. See Kessler, *Voices from Amsterdam*, ix–xxiv, and Bauer, *All diese Worte*, 56–104, and the Conclusion in this volume.

104. *Bijbels ABC*, 111.

Conclusion

1. See the discussion in chap. 1., "Career Struggles."

2. See chap. I, "Youth and Education," supra.

3. *Gecroonde Allemansgading* has an opening section entitled "Jeugdwerk" [Youth Work], subdivided in Bikoerim I and II (11–39); this represents his writings before his first pastorate.

4. In the thirties, but not published until 1948, as the first segment of *Levende Woord*. See n.41, chap. 1.

5. *Levende Woord*, 43.

6. *Bijbels ABC*, 11.

7. "He was an exceptionally reflective thinker; the main points of his work are not easily set out in a system." (Marquardt, *Bijbelse houding*, 33)

8. It is the final article in . . . *als een die dient* (346–348). He begins with the expression of sentiments reminiscent of St. Augustine: "I had gladly wanted to do very, very much [more] for you, for truly a little, oh, too little, have I loved you in Christ."

9. See n.14, chap. 1, for relevant information.

10. See n.6, chap. 1.

11. In a lecture on January 18, 1935, entitled "Heeft het Oude Testament voor ons nog betekenis? [Does the Old Testament still have Meaning For Us?]" Miskotte said: "No one but Harnack has said: 'In the second century, to reject the Old Testament would have been an error which the church rightly rejected, to retain it in the 16th century was a fate which the Reformation could not reject, but to maintain it in the 19th century as authoritative is the result of religious and ecclesiastical paralysis.'" (With thanks to Dr. D. Monshouwer, Director, The Miskotte Foundation, and Ms. Christiane Berkvens-Stevelinck, Curator of the Section "Westerse handschriften," Universiteitsbibliotheek, Leiden, for permission to read some of Miskotte's manuscripts.)

12. According to Mrs. E. Kuiper-Miskotte, in private conversation.

13. In his article "Christological Interpretation as a Way of 'Salvaging' the Old Testament? Wilhelm Vischer and Gerhard von Rad" in *Canon and Theology. Overtures to an Old Testament Theology* (Minneapolis: Fortress, 1993), Rolf Rendtorff writes about the influence of W. Vischer's book *Das Christuszeugnis des Alten Testament* (2 vols., Munich, 1934, and Zurich, 1942) in Germany. Rendtorff claims that when it came out (in Hitler's Germany) it entered "almost a complete vacuum"

(78). However, it served to stimulate Gerhard von Rad to study the Old Testament as a book of Judaism and Christianity.

14. See n.25, chap. 2.

15. Muis, *Openbaring,* 454, 455.

16. Interestingly, in January 1939, he published his *Het Gewone Leven* (on Ruth), and only six months latter his *Edda en Thora,* just before the beginning of World War II), as it were, counterbalancing each other. However, while his work on Ruth is only about Torah, *Edda en Thora* is not only about Germanic paganism but also about the Torah—his real concern. See also Dieuwke Parlevliet, "Het gewone leven als verzet [Common Life as Resistance]" in *Antwoord aan het nihilisme,* 29–36.

17. Like many Dutch, Miskotte seems to have had something of a love-hate feeling toward things German: "Like few others he realized being a partaker of Germanic culture, and saw threatening and barbaric paganism beginning to move like a tidal wave. I really know of no other theologian beside Karl Barth who was so involved with the problematic of the German people as was Miskotte—perhaps I should call him: Miskotte, *the* theologian of the resistance." (Marquardt, *Bijbelse houding,* 34)

18. It was during Miskotte's childhood that Adolf Harnack (1851–1930) published his influential *Das Wesen des Christentums* (1900). Harnack perhaps more than any anyone else epitomized the kind of liberal Christianity that Barth (and Miskotte with him) tried to counteract.

19. His son writes: "He felt himself called and obligated to put his gifts in the service of theology and church, but also to as many people as possible who were outside of the church." *Niet te vergeten Miskotte,* 84.

20. *When the Gods are Silent,* 17.

21. Karl Löwith, *From Hegel to Nietzsche. The Revolution in Nineteenth-Century Thought* (New York: Columbia University Press, 1964), 193.

22. See Mircea Eliade, *Cosmos and History. The Myth of the Eternal Return* (Harper Torchbook. New York: Harper & Row, 1959).

23. R. Oost, *Omstreden bijbeluitleg.* Bauer, *All diese Worte.* Kessler, *Voices from Amsterdam.* See n.19, chap. 5.

24. See Kessler, *Voices from Amsterdam,* "Introduction," ix–xxiv.

25. "Miskotte, inspirator, voortrekker [Miskotte, inspirer, pioneer]" in *De Bijbel maakt school* [The Bible goes Academic]. (Baarn: Ten Have, 1984), 83–91.

26. Three samples of his work are published in Kessler, *Voices from Amsterdam:* one methodological ("The Scope of a Small Literary Unit in the Old Testament," 37–51) and two exegetical: "The Way of Abraham," 95–112 and "'Because You have Hearkened to My Voice': Genesis 22" 113–130.

27. Breukelman, "Miskotte's inspiration: Tenach en dogmatiek (Miskotte's Inspiration: Tanakh and Dogmatics) in K. H. Miskotte et al., *De weg der verwachting,* 34.

28. Ibid., 37.

29. Ibid., 47, 48.

30. Ibid., 48.

31. Ibid., 50.

32. In response to pressure from students (who began to beat a path to his parsonage), he was offered a post at the University of Amsterdam, but he never received his doctorate, nor was he ever made Professor [hoogleraar].

33. Bijbelse Theologie I,1 Schrift-lezing [Biblical Theology I, 1 Scripture-Reading] (Kampen: J. H. Kok, 1980); *Bijbelse Theologie, III,1: De theologie van de*

evangelist Mattheüs. 1. De ouverture van het evangelie [Biblical Theology, III.1: The Theology of Matthew the Evangelist 1. The Overture of the Gospel] (Kampen: J. H. Kok, 1984); *Bijbelse Theologie I,2. De theologie van het Boek Genesis. Het eerstelingschap van Israël* [Biblical Theology I,2: The Theology of the Book of Genesis. Israel the Firstborn] (Kampen: J. H. Kok, 1992).

34. Kessler, *Voices from Amsterdam.*

Bibliography

Antwoord aan het nihilisme: met Miskotte op de weg der verwachting. Edited by K. Deurloo and René Venema. Baarn: Ten Have, 1994.

Asch, Scholem. *The Nazarene*. 1939.

Baeck, Leo. *Das Evangelium als Urkunde der jüdische Glaubensgeschichte*. 1938.

Barth, K. *Church Dogmatics,* I,1: The Doctrine of the Word of God. Edited by G. W. Bromiley and T. F. Torrance. Edinburgh: T. & T. Clark, 1975.

———. *Church Dogmatics,* I,2: The Doctrine of the Word of God. Edited by G. W. Bromiley and T. F. Torrance. Edinburgh: T. & T. Clark, 1956.

———. *Church Dogmatics,* II,2: The Doctrine of God. Edited by G. W. Bromiley and T. F. Torrance. Edinburgh: T. & T. Clark, 1957.

———. *The Word of God and the Word of Man*. New York: Harper & Row, 1957.

Bauer, Uwe F. W., All diese Worte. Impulse zur Schriftauslegung aus Amsterdam. Expliziert an der Schilfmeererzählung in Exodus 13,17–14,31. Frankfurt am Main: Peter Lang, 1991.

Bauer, Walter, et al. *A Greek-English Lexicon of the New Testament and Other Early Christian Literature*. Second edition. Chicago/London: University of Chicago Press, 1979.

De Bijbel maakt school: Een Amsterdamse weg in de exegese. Edited by K. A. Deurloo and R. Zuurmond. Baarn: Ten Have, 1984.

Boman, T. *Hebrew Thought Compared with Greek*. London: SCM Press, 1960.

Breukelman, F. *Bijbelse Theologie, I,1. Schriftlezing*. Kampen: J. H. Kok, 1980.

———. *Bijbelse Theologie, III,1. De theologie van de evangelist Mattheüs. 1. De ouverture van het evangelie*. Kampen: J. H. Kok, 1984.

———. *Bijbelse Theologie I,2. De theologie van het Boek Genesis. Het eerstelingschap van Israël*. Kampen: J. H. Kok, 1992.

Buber, Martin, *I and Thou*. Edinburgh: T. & T. Clark, 1937.

Buber, Martin and Franz Rosenzweig. *Die fünf Bücher der Weisung*. 4 vols. Stuttgart: Deutsche Bibelgesellschaft, 1992.

Calvin, John. *Institutes of the Christian Religion*. Translated by F. L. Battles. 2 vols. Philadelphia: Westminster Press, 1960.

Cranfield, C. E. B. *Romans. A Shorter Commentary*. Grand Rapids, Mich.: Wm. B. Eerdmans Publishing Company, 1985.

Dienstboek voor de Nederlandse Hervormde Kerk. The Hague: Boekencentrum, 1957.

Eliade, M. *Cosmos and History: The Myth of the Eternal Return*. New York: Harper, 1959.

Encyclopaedia Judaica. New York: Macmillan, 1971.

Gundry, R. H. *Matthew: A Commentary on His Literary and Theological Art*. Grand Rapids, Mich.: Wm. B. Eerdmans, 1982.

Gutzmann, Mathias. *Die Theologie von Kornelis Heiko Miskotte (1894–1976) in ihrem zeitgeschichtlichen und problemgeschichtlichen Kontext: Schriftliche Hausarbeit im Rahmen der Ersten Staatsprüfung für die Sekundarstufe II*. Paderborn: Gesamthochschule, 1993.

Die Hebräische Bibel und ihre zweifache Nachgeschichte: Festschrift für Rolf Rendtorff zum 65. Geburtstag. Edited by E. Blum et al. Neukirchen: Neukirchener Verlag, 1990.

Heschel, A. J. *The Prophets*. II. New York: Harper, 1962.

Horen en zien: Opstellen over de theologie van K. H. Miskotte. Edited by H. W. de Knijff and G. W. Neven. Kampen: J. H. Kok, 1991.

Jacob, E. *Theology of the Old Testament*. New York: Harper, 1958.

Johnson, A. R. *The One and the Many*. Cardiff: University of Wales Press, 1942.

Kittel, Gerhard et al. *Theological Dictionary of the New Testament: One volume edition*. Grand Rapids, Mich.: Wm. B. Eerdmans, 1985.

Klausner, Joseph. *Jesus of Nazareth*. New York: Macmillan, 1953.

———. *From Jesus to Paul*. New York: Macmillan, 1943.

Kohlbrügge, H. F. *Die Lehre des Heils*. Elberfeld, 1903.

Kornelis Heiko Miskotte (1894–1976); brug tussen cultuur & theologie. Edited by A. C. den Besten at al. Kampen: J. H. Kok, 1995.

Kruijf, G. G. de., *Heiden, Jood en Christen: Een studie over de theologie van K. H. Miskotte*. Baarn: Ten Have, 1981.

Levenson, J. D. *The Hebrew Bible, the Old Testament, and Historical Criticism: Jews and Christians in Biblical Studies*. Louisville: Westminster/Knox, 1993.

Liedboek voor de kerken. The Hague: Boekencentrum, 1978.

Löwith, K. *From Hegel to Nietzsche: The Revolution in Nineteenth-Century Thought*. New York: Columbia University Press, 1964.

Luther, Martin. *Commentary on the Romans*. Translated by J. T. Mueller. Grand Rapids Mich.: Kregel, 1993.

Margolis, Max L., and Alexander Marx. *A History of the Jewish People*. New York: Atheneum, 1969.

Miskotte, H. H. *Niet te vergeten Miskotte*. Kampen: J. H. Kok, 1981.

Miskotte, K. H. *Antwoord uit het onweer: Een verhandeling over het boek Job*. Amsterdam: Uitgeversmaatschappij Holland, 1936 = Verzameld Werk 10. Kampen: J. H. Kok, 1984.

———. *Als de goden zwijgen*. Amsterdam: Uitgeversmaatschappij Holland, 1956; 1965 second printing = Verzameld Werk 8. Kampen: J. H. Kok, 1984.

———. *ABC della Bibbia*. Brescia, 1981.

———. *Biblische Meditationen*. Munich: Chr. Kaiser, 1967.

———. *Biblisches ABC: Wider das unbiblische Bibellesen*. Neukirchen: Neukirchener Verlag, 1976.

———. *Bijbels ABC*. Nijkerk: Callenbach, 1941, 7th printing. Baarn: Ten Have, 1992.

———. *Edda en Thora: Een vergelijking van Germaansche en Israëlitische religie*.

Nijkerk: Callenbach, 1939; second printing = Verzameld werk 7. Kampen: J. H. Kok, 1983.

———. *Feest in de voorhof: Sermoenen voor randbewoners.* Amsterdam: Uitgeversmaatschappij Holland, 1951.

———. *Geloof en kennis: Theologische voordrachten.* Haarlem: Uitgeversmaatschappij Holland, 1966.

———. *Geloof bij de gratie Gods.* Amsterdam: Uitgeversmaatschappij Holland, 1938.

———. *Geschonken eindigheid.* Kampen: J. H. Kok, 1978.

———. *Gevulde stilte.* Kampen: J. H. Kok, 1974.

———. *Het gewone leven: In den spiegel van het boek Ruth.* Amsterdam: Uitgeversmaatschappij Holland, 1939 = Verzameld werk 10 Kampen: J. H. Kok, 1984.

———. *Gods vijanden vergaan: Preek 9 Mei 1945.* Amsterdam: Ten Have, 1945.

———. *Der Gott Israels und die Theologie: Ausgewählte Aufsätze.* Neukirchen: Neukirchener Verlag, 1975.

———. *Grensgebied.* Nijkerk: G. F. Callenbach, 1954.

———. *Hoofdsom der historie: Voordrachten over de visioenen van den apostel Johannes.* Nijkerk: G. F. Callenbach, 1945.

———. *In de gecroonde allemansgading: Keur uit het verspreide werk van Prof. Dr. K. H. Miskotte.* Edited by W. C. Snethlage and E. A. J. Plug. Nijkerk: G. F. Callenbach, 1946.

———. *In de waagschaal: Een keur uit de artikelen van Dr. K. H. Miskotte uit de eerste vijf jaargangen van In de Waagschaal* = Verzameld Werk 1. Kampen: J. H. Kok, 1982.

———. *In de waagschaal.* Edited by W. Barnard and Dr. J. J. Buskes. Amsterdam: Uitgeversmaatschappij Holland, 1960.

———. *Johannes Hermanus Gunning.* Rotterdam, 1941.

———. *Das Judentum als Frage an die Kirche.* Wuppertal, 1970.

———. *K. H. Miskotte, Karl Barth: Inspiratie en vertolking. Inleidingen, essays, briefwisseling.* Edited by A Geense et al. = Verzameld Werk 2. Kampen: J. H. Kok, 1987.

———. *De kern van de zaak: Toelichting bij een proeve van hernieuwd belijden.* Nijkerk: G. F. Callenbach, 1950.

———. *Miskende majesteit.* Nijkerk: G. F. Callenbach, 1969.

———. *Om de waarheid te zeggen: Opstellen over het kerkelijk belijden.* Kampen: J. H. Kok, 1971.

———. *Om het levende woord.* The Hague: Daamen, 1948; second printing: Kampen: J. H. Kok, 1973.

———. *Predigten aus vier Jahrzehnten.* Munich, 1969.

———. *The Roads of Prayer.* New York, 1968.

———. *Über Karl Barths Kirchliche Dogmatik: Kleine Präludien und Phantasien.* Theologische Existenz Heute, Neue Folge, 89, 1961.

———. *Uit de dagboeken 1917–1930,* Verzameld Werk 4. Kampen: J. H. Kok, 1985.

———. *Uit de dagboeken 1930–1934,* Verzameld Werk 5a. Kampen: J. H. Kok, 1990.

———. *Uitkomst: Toespraken voor jongeren van elke leeftijd.* Amsterdam: Uitgeversmaatschappij Holland, 1948.

———. *De vreemde vrijspraak.* Amsterdam: Uitgeversmaatschappij Holland, 1938.

———. *Der Weg des Gebets.* Munich: Chr. Kaiser, 1967.

———. *Wenn die Götter schweigen: Vom Sinn des Alten Testaments.* Munich: Chr. Kaiser, 1963, third printing, 1966.

———. *Het wezen der joodse religie: Vergelijkende studie over de voornaamste structuren der Joodse Godsdienstphilosophie van dezen tijd.* Amsterdam: Paris, 1932; second printing: Haarlem: Uitgeversmaatschappij Holland, 1964.

———. *When the Gods Are Silent.* Translated by J. W. Doberstein. New York / Evanston: Harper & Row, 1967.

———. *Zur biblischen Hermeneutik.* Theologische Studien, 55; Zollikon, 1959.

Muis, J. *Openbaring en interpretatie: Het verstaan van de Heilige Schrift volgens K. Barth en K. H. Miskotte.* The Hague: Boekencentrum, 1989.

Oberman, H. A. *The Roots of Anti-Semitism in the Age of Renaissance and Reformation.* Philadelphia: Fortress, 1981.

Om het levende woord: Bijbels-theologische en dogmatische uitgave van het Delenus-Instituut van de Faculteit der Godgeleerdheid Universiteit van Amsterdam. Kampen: J. H. Kok, 1994.

Oost, R. *Omstreden bijbeluitleg. Aspecten en achtergronden van de hermeneutische discussie rondom de exegese van het Oude Testament in Nederland.* Kampen: J. H. Kok, 1986.

Oxford Dictionary of the Christian Church. Edited by F. L. Cross et al. Oxford: Oxford University Press, 1990, rev. ed.

Pedersen, Johannes. *Israel: Its Life and Culture,* I,II. London: Oxford University Press, 1926, 1940.

Rad, G. von. *Old Testament Theology, II: The Theology of Israel's Prophetic Traditions.* New York: Harper & Row, 1965.

———. *Studies in Deuteronomy.* (Studies in Biblical Theology, 9). Chicago: Regnery, 1953.

Rendtorff, Rolf. "Christological Interpretation as a Way of 'Salvaging' the Old Testament? Wilhelm Vischer and Gerhard von Rad," in *Canon and Theology; Overtures to an Old Testament Theology.* Minneapolis: Augsburg Fortress, 1993.

Rosenzweig, F. *The Star of Redemption.* New York: Holt, Rinehart & Winston, 1970.

———. *Briefe.* 1935.

Sandmel, S. *A Jewish Understanding of the New Testament.* New York: Hebrew Union College Press, 1956.

———. *The Genius of Paul: A Study in History.* New York: Farrar, 1958.

Stoevesandt, H. *Karl-Barth-Kornelis Heiko Miskotte Briefwechsel 1924–1968.* Zurich: Theologisches Verlag, 1991.

Three Jewish Philosophers: Philo, Saadya Gaon, Jehudah Halevi. Edited by H. Lewy et al. New York: Meridian Books, 1960.

Tomson, P. T. "K. H. Miskotte und das heutige jüdisch-christliche Gespräch." *Nederlands Theologisch Tijdschrift* 44, 15–34.

Trepp, Leo. *Judaism: Development and Life.* Belmont, Calif.: Dickenson, 1966.

Van der Leeuw, G. *Religion in Essence and Manifestation: A Study in Phenomenology.* 2 vols. New York: Harper & Row, 1963.

Velden, Marinus J. G. van der. *K. H. Miskotte als prediker: Een homiletisch onderzoek.* The Hague: Boekencentrum, 1984.

Vischer, W. "Das Alte Testament und die Geschichte." *Zwischen den Zeiten,* 1921.

———. *Das Christuszeugnis des Alten Testaments,* 2 vols. Munich, 1964; Zurich, 1942.

Voices from Amsterdam: A Modern Tradition of Reading Biblical Narrative. Edited by Martin Kessler; Semeia Studies; Atlanta: Scholars Press, 1994.

Vriezen, Th. C. *Hoofdlijnen der Theologie van het Oude Testament.* Wageningen: Veenman, 1954.

De weg der verwachting. Edited by K. A. Deurloo. Baarn: Ten Have, 1975.

Woord en Wereld: Opgedragen aan Prof. Dr. K. H. Miskotte naar aanleiding van zijn aftreden als kerkelijk hoogleraar te Leiden op 14 december 1959. Edited by A. J. Rasker et al. Amsterdam: Arbeiderspers, 1961.

Wright, G. E. *God Who Acts: Biblical Theology as Recital.* Studies in Biblical Theology, 8; Chicago: Allenson, 1952.

Yeago, D. S. "The New Testament and the Nicene Dogma: A Contribution to the Recovery of Theological Exegesis." *Pro Ecclesia* 3 (1994): 152–164.

INDEX

SCRIPTURE INDEX

E 78